The Bundesliga Blueprint

How Germany became the Home of Football

Lee Price

Published in 2015 by Bennion Kearny Limited.

Copyright © Bennion Kearny 2015

ISBN: 978-1-910515-32-7

Published by Bennion Kearny Limited
6 Woodside
Churnet View Road
Oakamoor
ST10 3AE

www.BennionKearny.com

Acknowledgements
The people that made it happen

I have to say thank you to a long list of people for helping me make this book a reality. Obviously, as an Englishman, I needed experts from within the German game to offer their insight and support, which the following did.

A big thank you to…

…Carolin Kramer for facilitating my behind the scenes visit to Dortmund's training facility.

…Michael Ballack for committing to a 'five minute' interview, and giving me well over half an hour of his time, with both his honesty and sense of humour very welcome.

…Ron-Robert Zieler for making time for me in his few days off between Hannover's final game of the 2015 season and joining up with the Germany squad.

…Jens Nowotny for tolerating my inane jokes about English weather, and a questionable train signal.

…Christoph Kramer for testing my GCSE German when translating our conversation – it certainly wasn't as good as your English, which you were shy about.

…Rino Matarazzo for offering me a fascinating insight into youth football coaching amid his busy holiday preparations, and Luana Valentini for arranging the interview.

…Benjamin McFadyean for your insight into the world of a British-based Dortmund fan – likewise George Docherty and Matthew Gerrard. Thank you to John Baine for being so enthusiastic about St Pauli – good luck with your book.

…Meinolf Sprink at Leverkusen for being so helpful and patient, Steffi Pennekamp and Oliver Ruhnert at Schalke, Knut Stahmer and Osayamen Osawe at Halle, and Matthias Hack and Martin Hornberger of Paderborn.

…the BBC for allowing me to use quotes from an article authored by Jurgen Klinsmann in Chapter Two, and to Nick Harris at Sports Intelligence for permitting use of your fabulous research, as well as providing me with a few helpful pointers.

…BT Sport and Dan Tunna for your support with Owen Hargreaves' quotes.

…James Lumsden-Cook for your support with this book, and to Melanie Michael-Greer for believing in the idea. Clearly, I work well with people with double-barrelled names!

Table of Contents

Introduction   1
Chapter 1 The Disaster Tournament   5
Chapter 2 The 10-Year Plan   11
Chapter 3 The Jürgen Factor   29
Chapter 4 Jung, Löw: How Germany learned that you can   37
win things with kids
Chapter 5 Debt prevention rules, OK? The original   51
Financial Fair Play
Chapter 6 Fan frenzy: Fan = friend, see?   63
Chapter 7 Bor-illiant Dortmund   77
Chapter 8 Becoming a global phenomenon   89
Chapter 9 Bayern mighty: The global footballing colossus   103
with a conscience. Kinda.
Chapter 10 The best of the rest   121
Chapter 11 Culmination, coronation, jubilation   133
Chapter 12 Follow the Bundes-leaders: what the Premier   141
League can learn
Chapter 13 The downsides   163
Chapter 14 Conclusions   171

Introduction

5.28pm, 13th July 2014: Rio de Janeiro.

The young forward paced the sideline cautiously – gripped somewhere between anxiety and focus – before deliberately removing his orange bib following a nod from the manager.

With less than two minutes remaining on the clock, the 22-year-old wasn't being brought on for a token run-out, to kill time, he was being introduced to win the World Cup – at the expense of the tournament's all-time leading scorer, no less.

As Mario Götze prepared to take to the field, the legendary Miroslav Klose trudged off having failed to breach the resolute Argentinian backline. Götze's coach, perhaps sensing the youngster's apprehension, leaned in to offer some advice and encouragement.

"Show the world you are better than [Lionel] Messi and can decide the World Cup," Joachim Löw urged.

No pressure then, son.

But this wasn't any old wonderkid that was being introduced to the fray. This was a young man who had been at the very heart of Germany's '10-year plan' to rebuild themselves as an international force after the humiliation of Euro 2000 – most likely the first tournament Götze will remember watching, then eight-years-old.

In that European Championships, with a line-up including greats such as Lothar Matthäus, Oliver Bierhoff and Mehmet Scholl, Germany crashed out of the group stage without mustering a single victory – even finishing below a faltering England – and scoring just once, an equaliser against Romania to secure their only point.

The German game had reached its lowest ebb.

Despite such crushing disappointment, Götze was clearly inspired; within months, he'd joined the youth academy of Borussia Dortmund, having moved to the Ruhr area two years earlier, as his professor father took a job at the local university.

Introduction

With BVB, he progressed rapidly through the ranks of youth football – suddenly the recipient of renewed focus, funding, and footing in the German game – and quickly emerged as the brightest star of his generation. Four years before his decisive substitute appearance in Rio, Matthias Sammer, the FA's Technical Director, hailed Götze as "one of the best talents Germany has ever had".

Despite his tender years and slender shoulders, by the time of the Brazil World Cup, the so-called 'German Messi' was well versed in thriving under pressure. He'd already lifted three Bundesliga titles, reached a Champions League final, and completed a controversial £31.5million switch between his homeland's biggest clubs – prompting accusations that he'd abandoned Dortmund for Bayern Munich, drawing the crowd's ire upon subsequent returns to the Westfalenstadion.

At the age of just 18, he was leading Dortmund to a Bundesliga title, and becoming a full Germany international, all while still living at home with his parents. This was a talent undaunted.

So it was, perhaps, little surprise that, when the substitute found himself free in the opposition box in the latter stages of extra time, Götze was able to coolly chest a left-wing cross into his path and volley home a goal he will never, ever be allowed to forget.

As delirium set in all around him, and he was mobbed by overjoyed teammates, Götze's face was almost expressionless – either he was in complete shock, or this was simply part of the plan all along.

Or, more likely, a bit of both. Post-match, as commentators hailed 'Super Mario' and his coach dubbed him 'the miracle boy', Götze's reaction was telling: "It is an unbelievable feeling. You score that goal and you don't really know what's happening."

But his manager did. For Löw, who joined the national set-up after another ill-fated European Championships in 2004 – initially as assistant manager, before stepping up to head coach two years later when Jürgen Klinsmann resigned – this was the culmination of the project he'd been so central to.

In fact, since 2004, Germany had reached at least the semi-finals of every major international tournament they'd entered – including the final of Euro 2008, where they fell short against a rampant Spain side in their prime.

After such steady improvement and relative over-achievement, Löw knew they were due some success in Brazil: "We've made constant progress and believed in the project. If any group deserves it, it's this team."

But it wasn't just the national team that were reaping the benefits – rather, this was the crowning glory of German football's brilliant resurrection. Barely a year earlier, fans and pundits alike quipped that 'football's coming home' as an all-German Champions League final took place at Wembley, acting as a symbolic passing of the torch between the game's spiritual homes past and present.

If England's Premier League is feted globally for its drama and riches, Germany's Bundesliga has gone about establishing a rather different reputation: there, it's not just the players who are handsomely rewarded by football, but supporters too. It is widely considered the most fan-friendly division in the sport, with attendances soaring, and topping the figures achieved in England.

In global sport, only the NFL can boast a better average attendance than the Bundesliga – which attracted 42,609 fans per game of the 2013/14 season. The Premier League's corresponding figure, by comparison, was 36,695.

Little wonder the German model on and off the pitch has been increasingly hailed as the ultimate – with a focus on youth development, healthy and responsible finances, and with supporters made a priority not a commodity.

Here, in *The Bundesliga Blueprint* we shall trace German football's road to redemption – from the emergency plan of action drawn up in the summer of 2000 that would become the country's guideline for success, to the £1.5million top-secret facility at which the World Cup winning goal was 'born'. A lot of the insight gained will come via access inside the club that came to symbolise the footballing revolution so perfectly, Dortmund.

If England is ever to regain its claim as the home of football – and, indeed, challenge for international success – there is much we can learn from our German counterparts.

Chapter 1
The Disaster Tournament

Inspired, perhaps, by a desire for neatness, many observers ear-mark Euro 2004 as the beginning of Germany's '10 year plan' – with fans of German stereotypes about efficiency suitably pleased that the national team's success came about exactly a decade later at the 2014 World Cup.

But, while Germany's success at Brazil 2014 prompted the mass media to revisit Euro 2004 gleefully – the 10-year plan delivered to perfection – the timing of that schedule was a little bit out. It was actually in 2000, in Belgium and Holland, where true ignominy was suffered, and where the German game reached its nadir.

Though they were drawn in an admittedly tricky group alongside Portugal, England and Romania, Germany went into the tournaments as favourites to proceed, and top seeds in the group. Portugal had only qualified as best runner-up, while England had relied on the play-offs to squeak through.

Given that, only opening round opponents and rank outsiders Romania had actually won their qualifying group – surprisingly finishing ahead of Portugal – and they were expected to be easy prey for the reigning European Champions anyway. But the holders were caught cold, as Viorel Moldovan gave Romania a shock lead after just five minutes. It was to set the tone for the rest of the tournament. Mehmet Scholl's sweetly struck equaliser earned Germany a barely deserved point, and saved some face, but their performance was unconvincing – even the official UEFA match report described it as 'abject'. And that was to be as good as it got.

Their second fixture was against England, the opponent they'd memorably vanquished in the semi-finals of their Euro 1996 success, but this Germany side were well beaten – captain Alan Shearer's flying header providing the Three Lions with a semblance of revenge.

Chapter 1

It prompted assertions in the media that Erich Ribbeck's men were a spent force, lacking the star quality of years gone by. Even so, Germany could still progress to the quarter-finals – all they had to do was see off the already qualified Portugal, and hope England lost to Romania by a closer margin.

But, while the latter permutation played into their hands, Germany were resoundingly thumped by a much rotated Portugal line up, Sérgio Conçeicao's hat trick giving the largely second string XI a comfortable victory – and, perhaps, the most jarring result of a bleak tournament. Even an early Christian Chivu goal for Romania against England couldn't spark life into a dismal German performance. The holders had been sent home early, having mustered just a single goal, finishing rock bottom of Group A after a trio of meek displays.

But what exactly happened? And why was it so bad when, just two years later, what was predominantly the same side went on to reach a World Cup final? To investigate further, I spoke to Michael Ballack – the brightest and, for some, only star of that generation – and Jens Nowotny, the bruising centre half who was Ballack's team mate at Leverkusen, and a fellow tournament first-timer in 2000.

That debutant novelty soon wore off, though, as Ballack – on the back of an impressive debut campaign at Leverkusen, where he inspired them to second in the Bundesliga, desperately close to an unlikely title – joined a squad fraught with infighting amongst both the playing and coaching staff. It wasn't the ideal environment for a wet-behind-the-ears rookie, despite his initial excitement at playing alongside the 39-year-old veteran Lothar Matthäus, a genuine giant of German football history.

He recalled: "The team was split. When Erich Ribbeck took over, he brought Lothar Matthäus back into the team – and not everyone was happy with that decision. Matthäus had not been involved in 1998 with Berti Vogts, so he was quite a lot older. I remember, as a young player, it was interesting to see how the older group – players like Linke, Hamann, Jeremies, Ziege – were quite powerful.

"And we were not really 100% convinced of the coach – he was a nice guy, but there was a power struggle with his assistant, Uli Stielike. We didn't know who was the boss. Stielike was put in temporary charge before Ribbeck was introduced on top of him.

"So that was the start of a quite difficult time, in terms of power – who actually trains the team, who's the head coach – you always had the feeling that they didn't work really well together. And the team is very sensitive to this kind of relationship. So when, at the top of the team, there is something wrong, obviously it goes down to the players. On top of that, it was not a strong group; there were a lot of groups within the team.

"The pre-tournament preparation in Mallorca was bad. We broke up some training sessions because of disagreements in terms of tactics, how we played, the intensity of training. For me as a young player, it was a good experience – not in terms of how it was, but how it should have been.

"So when we started Euro 2000, we weren't in the best condition, which you could see on the pitch. It was a tough group with England and Portugal, but still Germany should perform well.

"But the confidence in the group wasn't good, already before we started, so overall it wasn't the best period to start the tournament, with high expectations, which a country always puts into a national team."

It is clear from the way he discusses the tournament that Ballack is still disappointed by what happened at Euro 2000 – he sighed frequently when talking through what happened, in contrast to his otherwise upbeat patter throughout the rest of the conversation. His sense of humour, in particular, was a welcome surprise. But it would take a heavy dose of schadenfreude to jest about his experiences that summer.

For teammate Nowotny, it was difficult to understand how his first international tournament had ended in such disappointment and failure, having played all three games at Euro 2000, but he too pointed the finger at factions within the camp.

"There were some great players in the squad, like Lothar Matthäus, and for me, as my first international tournament, it was all new. Our opening game was a draw with Romania, which was disappointing, but a draw in the group stage is okay. Then we lost to England, but still had a chance to go through if we beat Portugal.

Chapter 1

"But they beat us 3-0, and that was a big disappointment. It made a huge discussion in Germany about what went wrong – was Matthäus too old? Were the players fit enough? Were they good enough?

"For me, it was simply that we didn't play as a team. It was like we were two teams in one – the defence and the offence. We were too many individual stars and not enough of a collective. We should have done better with the squad we had, but couldn't create a team on the field. We had a very smart trainer, Erich Ribbeck, and a good squad. It was hard to know what had gone wrong."

The fall-out from this failure was widespread, with fans, media and the German game's governing body all drawing conclusions and producing plans of action. But how did this national discourse affect a squad mostly based in Germany, with virtually no place to hide from the criticism?

Ballack recalled the chaos of the immediate aftermath – as the post Euro 2000 backlash got into full flow – and the initial pressures of the subsequent 10-year plan on young stars like him and Sebastian Deisler, the poster-boys of the time.

"After the disaster of 2000, there was a taskforce to find a new coach, because Ribbeck stepped back – or they fired him, I can't really remember – and the first decision of the new plan was 'who should train the national team'.

"I remember 'Christoph Daum should do it' and he was in discussions and then his thing with the cocaine came out – so it wasn't the best time overall for German football. I was a young player, too, and after Euro 2000 wasn't the best experience – my first tournament with the national team – it meant there was this expectation on younger players.

"The quality of the squad of the national team was not comparable to the talent of the team we have now. Every nation has periods when you have strong or better players, then maybe you have not so talented periods, and that was the case around 2000.

"We had to pay more attention to the youth players, because you could see the difference in technique, speed, and beautiful football internationally. Everyone knew that would take time, but those were the circumstances. The DFB were convinced we had to change something and, of course, they paid more attention to the young players; we were more involved.

"But, on the other side, that brought with it a certain kind of pressure. Normally, when you're 20, 21 – and I remember there were a few players around me as well – it doesn't help everyone immediately to get the attention. It comes with criticism. If you're young, you need time to grow – you're not just a Bundesliga player; to play for a national team is another step, and another level to compete with the best players in the world.

"So that means you need a little bit of experience as well, and you need to grow next to experienced players – but we didn't have these kinds of players who were stable and untouchable for the national team. It was a tricky situation for younger players, but you have to represent German football, and go through that type of situation."

That young team's growth, to the team we know and admire now, is such that the state of German football in 2000 is difficult to grasp in the context of the world-beating national team and envy-inducing Bundesliga of today. England has long feared Germany internationally but even the Three Lions were able to look down on their traditional rivals in the aftermath of Euro 2000 – recording that now legendary 5-1 victory a year later. As Die Mannschaft appeared to be in free-fall, a side led by Emile Heskey was able, inexplicably, to run riot in Munich.

What followed, though, was to be a complete reversal with German football undergoing a thorough overhaul. Their footballing authorities would produce an era-defining plan, the contents of which would later become gospel for under-performing nations looking for a manuscript to rebuild with. Amongst those citing the Germans' plan as inspiration, of course, were England…

Chapter 2
The 10-Year Plan

In 2010, shortly after the South Africa World Cup, where Germany finished third, the Bundesliga produced a 45-page document entitled '10 Years of Academies: Talent pools of top-level German football', to celebrate the progress enjoyed since Euro 2000.

The front of the brochure stars a triumvirate of poster-boys for the German success story – Thomas Müller, Mario Götze, and a very young looking Manuel Neuer.

The tone isn't boastful – that would be about as unGerman as spending £60million on a substitute – but there's a definite sense of pride throughout, as evidenced in the foreword, written by President of the League Association, Dr Reinhard Rauball, who had taken the helm three years earlier: "Most lately this superior performance by our national team has shown that the measures decided upon by the League Association and the 36 professional clubs in Germany ten years ago were correct.

"For all clubs, the compulsory introduction of academies for young players in 2001 was the building block which laid the way to a successful future for German football.

"The German youth policy is internationally recognised as the model to be aspired to, and has even been most recently cited by UEFA as the best in Europe. The times in which we had to look appreciatively to France, Spain or the Netherlands have passed.

"The provisos laid down in the licensing from the sporting, medical and pedagogical fields, combined with a unique philosophy for every academy, guarantee an integral education of young players – and ensure that these youngsters also have a future outside of football."

The shock of Euro 2000, the trauma of which is recounted in *Chapter 1*, reverberated around the German game, with the leading powers taking immediate and decisive action. Rather than hiding away from

11

their problems, they were tackled head-on, with no mincing of words.

This is demonstrated perfectly by one brutally honest heading in the celebratory Bundesliga brochure: "The bitter first-round defeat at Euro 2000 was the key moment: at the turn of the millennium German football stared disaster in the face – it completely lacked a professional foundation."

The reaction was instant, and extended far beyond merely sacking the manager – although Erich Ribbeck actually jumped before he was pushed, with his resignation announced the morning after Germany's hammering by Portugal, before his squad began the journey home from Belgium and Holland, and before his bosses could beat him to it.

Bundesliga clubs and the DFB declared a state of emergency. The nation's leading sides teamed up with the German FA – in contrast to the loggerheads usually witnessed between the Premier League's elite and the footballing bodies at Wembley over England duty – and demanded a radical rethink to the country's footballing approach.

Those involved in these high level discussions were particularly inspired by the model adopted by then World and European champions France, and their national football centre Clairefontaine. Some 30 miles southwest of Paris, it had become the true capital of French football, and the envy of every other international body on the planet.

A footballing world wonder, if you will.

This elite academy, which produced the likes of Nicolas Anelka, Louis Saha, and William Gallas, also likely inspired the timeframe of the DFB's plan. Clairefontaine was opened in 1988, and France lifted the World Cup exactly a decade later, with a side that included Clairefontaine graduate, and future all-time leading scorer, Thierry Henry.

A German task force was quickly established, with the French success story no doubt ringing in their ears. They were under no illusions: Germany needed its own Clairefontaine. But that task force didn't settle for a single academy – instead, they demanded 18.

The ambitious programme they came up with made it compulsory for Bundesliga clubs to have a youth academy; otherwise they would lose their license, and therefore their place in the professional game, from the 2001/02 season. A year later, this stipulation was extended to the second division, too, meaning 36 full-time academies would be in place. There was no messing about – even Germany 'fluking' their way to a World Cup final in 2002 couldn't deviate them from their plan.

In 2001, the Academies Committee was formed to manage the new legislation that had been brought in, and to ensure that young German talent was no longer being wasted – their job was to secure these kids' futures, whether that was in the game or not. This is best reflected in the strong, educational focus of the policies that were brought into place. Whereas English prodigies often abandon their school lives entirely in pursuit of footballing dreams, the German model demanded equal focus on education in the classroom and on the training pitch. Christian Seifert, formerly Chief Executive Officer of the DFL – the German Football League – explained this sensible, almost cautious, approach: "For a long time after the Bosman ruling, the situation was such that more and more players from abroad were obliged to come to Germany and young German talent barely had a chance.

"The combination of a career in football with a school education or vocational training is elementary. Only a very few young talents actually make the final leap into professional football. We therefore consider it our social responsibility to provide youngsters, even outside of football, with the best possible education.

"That more young boys from the (youth) academies go on to a grammar school than the national average shows that this aspect of education is also taken very seriously indeed." So much so that 'do not neglect school' is a nationally recognised mantra throughout the football league's academies. At many clubs, changing room boards display which team has achieved the best results over the past six months – that's *school* results, not footballing ones. For German Academies, the educational league tables are on a level pegging with the footballing standings – at least until the players come of age.

On the pitch, the Academies Committee decided to move away from the Dutch model of standardising certain playing styles. Instead, their key objective was to simply produce an environment that would allow young players to thrive.

So, to be issued with a license, clubs were told that they had to hire full-time youth coaches and that the respective qualifications of these coaches would be a key contributing factor in how the club's academy would be graded. In a three-star evaluation system, conducted annually by an external agency on behalf of the DFL, the higher your youth system's rating, the more funding you receive from the league. This financial incentive was rerouted from the Champions League coffers for clubs who fail to qualify for the competition – UEFA's so-called Solidarity Fund – with a three-star academy promised additional revenues of at least €300,000 a year.

The certification visits, instigated in 2007 after being created at the University of Brussels, and carried out by the Double PASS team, evaluate everything from the clubs' playing fields and facilities, to staff members, via the club's philosophy, principles and education concepts for young players.

The eight areas upon which an academy is scrutinised are:

1. Strategy and Finances

2. Organisation and Procedure

3. Football Education and Evaluation

4. Support and Training

5. Personnel

6. Communication and Co-operation

7. Infrastructure and Facilities

8. Effectiveness and Permeability

Other stipulations include a demand for appropriate training grounds to be built, the establishment of a medical department, and co-operation with local schools for the educational arm of the new model – schooling was just as much a focus in the 10-year plan, as it is considered an irrelevance by English prodigies eager to just get on with being millionaire superstars already.

To support this, the DFB invested millions in basic training and fee-based coaches – putting their money where their mouth was, as it were.

Gerhard Mayer-Vorfelder, incoming President of the Football Association at the time of the sweeping changes in 2001, spelt out the benefits of this with no little glee on the 10-year anniversary of the blueprint.

He revelled: "We can be really proud of our youth work in Germany. Within ten years, the number of young players in the Bundesliga doubled. Today, these players edge each other out in the national team thanks to their fantastic education at the academies.

"You could say that we have almost perfected the promotion of young and elite talent in Germany. In former times, France and the Netherlands were the ultimate in this area – but we have long outstripped them.

"We managed to create 400 centres for the promotion of talent across the whole of Germany and, after the 2006 World Cup, built over 1,000 mini pitches. They were milestones. I have always said that these mini pitches replace street football, which you no longer find these days. You learn football there.

"The U19 Bundesliga, followed shortly afterwards by the U17 Bundesliga, was also part of the establishment of the talent promotion programme and the academies.

"It was furthermore decided to give scouting a higher priority in the international organisations. And the clubs entered into cooperation agreements with the 29 elite football schools. Players such as Mesut Özil, Toni Kroos, Jérôme Boateng, Mario Gómez graduated from one of these schools.

"The academies and training centres actually make a big contribution to integration. On the pitch, it doesn't matter whether you come from North Africa, Turkey or Germany. And as German is spoken on the pitch, integration comes easier to these youngsters, who learn the language more quickly and to a more competent level.

"We developed our own programme for primary schools... [in non-academy schools] staff are almost exclusively female and who have rather less to do with football."

Chapter 2

Former Chairman of the Academies Committee, Andreas Rettig, adds explanation to this potentially controversial point: "It is an absolutely fundamental problem that physical education lessons at school are being reduced more and more and that, as a result, children and young people are getting less and less exercise.

"The significance of sport in schools has dramatically decreased whilst the importance of all-day schools is on the increase.

"What is also important is that physical education is not taught by non-specialist teachers. Only with an educated P.E. teacher can the pupils' enthusiasm for the lessons taught be guaranteed."

The Academies initiative was a smart, all-encompassing plan of attack, which prioritised footballing success over being politically correct – could you imagine an English FA chief bold enough to announce that young players in the UK should only communicate in English? Within minutes, they'd most likely find themselves linked with the latest far-right political party in vogue, and their career in tatters.

And would you not expect gasps if you heard a government minister for sport daring to suggest that the disproportionate number of female primary school teachers might be having an impact on how young British boys enjoy P.E.? Accusations of sexism would overwhelm the individual bold enough to pipe up, until they backtracked and their suggestion was withdrawn, their common sense banished by the Twitter police.

But, clearly, the environment in Germany is less reactive and volatile – and the entirely sensible suggestions had the desired impact. Taking the example of integration, Mesut Özil is of Turkish descent, but has never wavered in his dedication to Germany – winning the 2010 Bambi award for being a 'prime example of successful integration within German society'.

Meanwhile, the young players emerging from German academies, regardless of background, are achieving increasingly impressive school results; the majority, whether they are German, German with a migration background, or foreigners, attend grammar school. That's above the national average for every category, which is an impressive achievement. From these results, some may conclude that footballers in Germany are 'smarter' than their peers, which is in stark contrast to the stereotype of their British contemporaries, who are perceived to be unable to string two sentences together.

The refreshingly honest approach to improving young players' footballing chances isn't the only difference between the British and German games, with Andreas Rettig illustrating another key disparity: "The biggest mistakes in football are often the result of temporary hype. In that respect, we cannot let ourselves be blinded by the recent outstanding successes of young players in the Bundesliga and the national team. We cannot allow complacency to set in."

Although Rettig was simply outlining the key approach to prolonged success in Germany, he could have just as easily been laying into the typical English reaction to a new starlet that has performed well for barely half a season. We've all been guilty of it, whether it's been with Jermaine Pennant, who cost Arsenal £2million at the age of 15, the injury-prone Kieron Dyer, the Premier League's youngest goal-scorer James Vaughan, or the quintessential example of failing to living up to the hype, Francis Jeffers.

That's not to say that the Bundesliga hasn't had its own premature flavours of the month, but the league's approach is more cautious – and, given that players remain in school until the age of 18, wunderkinds tend to be more balanced individuals.

Having juggled full-time education with a full-on training schedule, and with homework eating up much of their free time, young talents that progress into a Bundesliga first-team have more than earned their opportunity. It also means that they are well prepared should their footballing dream disappear.

As Rettig explains: "The interaction between education and football is, and will remain, an important theme. It must be possible in Germany that a young footballer can pursue a Bundesliga career whilst at the same time doing his A-levels."

Dr Uwe Harttgen, formerly Director of the Werder Bremen Academy, adds further explanation to the logical approach: "It is very important that the demands made on young people in education or employment go hand in hand with those of professional football. It is necessary to continually provide the players with new incentives, off and on the pitch.

Chapter 2

"We have observed that success in school also results in good performances on the pitch. This is why we want to offer the boys the best possible environment in which to grow.

"Even if this two-track education model requires sacrifices from the players, who then have only little free time, school education is, up to a certain age, more important than football.

"This is why we try to give players room to breathe and other opportunities to use their spare time alongside their school and football commitments.

"It's very important to us that they can decide freely how they want to spend their leisure time. Obviously, it hasn't escaped our attention that many young players enjoy computer games. As long as this doesn't get out of hand, it's entirely acceptable."

One of the successful initiatives introduced at Harttgen's Bremen was an after school club offering homework help sessions for members of the academy, maintaining the constant presence of the football club in all areas of the players' lives. It is an approach that is commonplace across the country, but how do clubs make the 'distraction' of schooling work in their training of future stars?

One of the best placed people to answer that question is Jürgen Gelsdorf, head of Bayer Leverkusen's youth academy – who was one of just three full-time youth coaches before Euro 2000. Now, eighty people work at the academy or Leistungszentrum (LZ) elite school, including an Educational Head, who is supported by five members of staff who generally work as teachers.

Gelsdorf explained: "We are focusing on a dual approach. We are focused on the sports education but also on the intellectual education because everybody is aware that, out of the 160 players who are enrolled in our academy right now, only a few will get a spot on our team – or will become professional football players.

"We want to educate the personality of the youth players as well as their sports performance by living up to values like team spirit, fair play, and partnership."

The 80 members of staff at Leverkusen – full-time, part-time, and volunteers – work with young talents who join the academy having been spotted by junior scouts. The emphasis is on locality.

"We are looking in the junior academy more or less from a local or regional standpoint. Most of the young players are coming from the vicinity, and are very proud to wear the Bayer 04 jersey. The emotional link between these players and our supporters is very high.

"Leverkusen is a small city surrounded by Cologne, Düsseldorf and very close to the Ruhr Valley – so we have the feeling of a small village, which is part of our DNA.

"The likes of René Adler, Gonzalo Castro and Stefan Reinartz have made it into the first team, underlining the strong connections with our supporters, because they have become local heroes."

But not every local lad will make it that far – between 12 and 15, coaches decide whether a player can advance to the next level, or whether he has to leave the academy. At least, in Germany, that shattered teen has a strong education to fall back on.

In general, the 10-year plan had succeeded: in the 2002/03 season, just 50% of all Bundesliga players were German. Ten years on from the revamp, and this figure climbed to 57%, while achieving 71% in the second tier. The average age of all players deployed in the Bundesliga also fell by 1.32 years, from 27.09 to 25.77.

By 2010, German football could boast 282 youth teams in the academies of professional clubs, with almost 5,500 young talents being nurtured between the ages of 11 and 22 by 433 coaches. Such players are known as 'local players' – educated by the club – and made up a fifth of the German club roster in 2010, soaring from 15% in 2007.

*

Of course, the German FA's 10-year plan was given further financial and motivational impetus by Germany winning the right to host the 2006 World Cup, with the announcement coming barely a month after their calamitous showing at Euro 2000.

Its impact is of particular significance given that 'Germany 2006' almost never was. Oceania delegate Charlie Dempsey abstained from voting, when he initially intended to vote against the German bid, which would have resulted in a tie with South Africa. Had he done so, FIFA President Sepp Blatter would have decided matters – and he was a public supporter of South Africa. Instead, Germany won the process, and reaped the benefits.

At the very least, it spared them an arduous qualification process, which would surely have relied heavily on wise, old heads to get them through. Instead, Germany were given the freedom to experiment and develop a new identity.

Indeed, Jürgen Klinsmann, upon being appointed as manager shortly after Euro 2004, was quick to highlight the tournament as his focus, stating before his inaugural fixture in charge, a friendly with Austria: "It's essential that we think long term about 2006... Of course, we want to beat Austria, we want to play good football, we want to see a good match but what really matters is the World Cup and nothing else."

Senior players such as Dietmar Hamann and Fredi Bobic were left out of the squad, while goalkeeper Oliver Kahn lost his captaincy and was sidelined, despite winning the Golden Ball four years earlier – the first goalkeeper in history to do so. Klinsmann seemed ready to implement his – and the FA's – plan without any sentiment. Nine of the final 23-man squad he named for the German World Cup were 24 or younger, with the batch of youth including 21-year-olds Bastian Schweinsteiger, Per Mertesacker, and Lukas Podolski – plus 22-year-old Philipp Lahm. Not all of the prodigious inclusions went on to become international mainstays – 22-year-old Mike Hanke won just 12 caps, while same-aged David Odonkor earned 16. Meanwhile, Robert Huth, then 21, first choice centre back and with Chelsea, went on to pick up only 19 caps after falling from grace during the tournament.

Ten players under 24 were included in the Euro 2008 squad, with 22-year-old Mario Gómez the stand-out future star, while the 2010 World Cup party boasted 12 – as Mesut Özil, Thomas Müller, Manuel Neuer, Sami Khedira, Holger Badstuber, Toni Kroos, and Jérôme Boateng all emerged together – the spine of a future force.

Mario Götze, Marco Reus and Mats Hummels were part of the 14 young stars selected for Euro 2012, with the squad maturing perfectly in time for Brazil 2014, where nine of the World Cup winning squad were under 24 – five of whom played a part in the final – while 24-year-old Marco Reus was a part of the original party, until injury ruled him out at the last moment.

The average age of the World Champions was an impressive 25.7, with 36-year-old record goal-scorer Miroslav Klose, captain Lahm (30), and back-up goalkeeper Roman Weidenfeller (33) the only squad members not in their twenties.

By contrast, the disaster of Euro 2000 included just two players of such youth – Michael Ballack, then 23, and the 20-year-old Sebastian Deisler, who would end up as the closest equivalent Germany had to Francis Jeffers, his immense promise unfulfilled. There were also nine thirty-somethings, one of whom, Lothar Matthäus, was only months away from his 40th birthday.

The same number of elder statesmen remained for the similarly disappointing 2004 Euros – but this time alongside six under-24s – though only four were given any game time.

With the 10-year plan well in progress, and approaching its halfway point, it is no coincidence that the 2006 squad boasted a refreshed look, which would prove to be a building block for future success – this young team would benefit from the tournament experience offered. And that experience would prove to be a positive one, as Germany were generally considered to have over-achieved – finishing third, only denied a place in the final by an extra time defeat to eventual winners Italy.

A 21-year-old, Lukas Podolski, scored both goals in the first knockout round victory over Sweden, adding to his group stage winner against Ecuador, as he was named Best Young Player of the tournament. Also 21, Bastian Schweinsteiger grabbed a brace in the third place playoff victory over Portugal, while Phillip Lahm (22) scored the tournament's opening goal and was named man of the match in Germany's second group game – a late, tense victory over Poland.

Even though they'd actually gone a spot better four years earlier – finishing as runner up at the 2002 World Cup, in-between back-to-back European Championships that were deemed disastrous – it is the 2006 tournament that is held up as the success story that kick-started the German re-emergence. And don't take my word for it – that is the verdict of players themselves.

Michael Ballack, the standout star of the Germany squad for so many years, hailed the impact of hosting a World Cup on what was a beleaguered squad at the time: "When the decision came out that Germany would get the World Cup, it was a big high – everyone knew then we had to represent Germany really well in our own country. It gave everyone – coaches, young players – a big target and motivation to be in that team: to be involved and to represent Germany.

"It was a great atmosphere, and a great World Cup. We went out a little bit unluckily against the world champions, but we improved our picture that we sent to the world – the way we played football was better than 2002 when we reached the final."

And current Borussia Mönchengladbach midfielder Christoph Kramer – who, at 23, started the 2014 World Cup final, but was withdrawn early on with concussion – was also quick to highlight the significance of that tournament.

He told me: "There has been a boost in Germany since the 2006 World Cup, and especially now with the World Cup title. In all of the youth academies, football is booming and is totally popular. I think that we, the younger players, just have to take advantage.

"Giving young players a chance is the German philosophy because, from our own ranks, especially in the transfer fees and salaries which the players are paid, are not so expensive.

"I have never seen so many well-educated young players with World Cup experience as there is now in Germany in abundance. You have really good players available at a low price.

"This used to be a bit different, but nowadays the players are already in the youth specialised training courses at the age of six, and training four or five times a week. They are so well-trained that I see no risk of them not getting into the first team."

*

Off the pitch, footballing facilities across the country received huge investment before the 2006 World Cup – Bayern Munich's impressive and now iconic Allianz Arena was built for the tournament, hosting the opening match, Germany's 4-2 defeat of Costa Rica. In turn, Schalke's Veltins-Arena was opened in 2001, amid the country's footballing shake up.

A slew of other sporting facilities were also developed and expanded for the World Cup, with changes geared towards practicality and efficiency rather than extravagance. Examples include 1899 Hoffenheim's widely admired 'El Dorado' training complex, and the brand new Kurtekotten facility opened by Bayer Leverkusen.

This is in addition to the German Football League's guidelines for the facilities that member clubs should have, which stipulate that Bundesliga clubs must have a training compound with changing rooms and three grass pitches, as well as artificial pitches, two of which must be lit with floodlights. Bundesliga 2 clubs are expected to have two pitches, at least one of which should have floodlights.

In each case, clubs are expected to establish a technical course, and facilitate indoor training during the winter. There must also be room for medical and physiotherapy applications adjacent to the changing rooms of the teams and coaches. Also compulsory are treatment rooms, massage rooms, saunas and relaxation baths.

*

Flashy PowerPoint presentations and endless meetings are all well and good, but much of this brave new plan of Germany relied on their players subscribing to it. So what was the reaction from within the dressing room? Having already been humiliated in Euro 2000, and torn lumps out of by the media and most of the nation, was the 10-year plan yet another blow for an already dejected squad of players?

Not in the way that stalwart Jens Nowotny – a Germany regular between 1997 and 2006 – recalled it: "In 2004, the team was an old team. That was changed after the tournament, we started to go for the youth – before, in 2000, it had only really been Sebastian Deisler.

"Many young players were brought in because Jürgen Klinsmann installed Per Mertesacker, Christoph Metzelder, and Robert Huth. He turned to young players to give them a chance to join the team for the 2006 World Cup.

"But soccer is a daily business – anything can happen, as we learnt from reaching the final of the 2002 World Cup. So us older players weren't demotivated or annoyed. We knew that our problem was consistency – we had the title in Euro 1996, but then in France 1998 we went out to Croatia. Then we were good in 2002, but had two disaster European Championships around it.

"We had the same situation as England, Holland, Portugal, and France. Every team goes through a bad time and then comes back. So, in Germany, we wanted to make a plan. It didn't matter that it was for ten years, because Germany is always a good team – but, instead, it took the pressure off the players and the situation now."

And didn't it work out perfectly for them? The courage shown by the DFB in 2000, when their national team was at its lowest ebb, not to react conservatively and with short-termism has been rewarded spectacularly.

Certainly, there must have been a temptation early on in the project to scrap it, and change the focus, particularly amongst initial failures such as the next European Championships, fully four years into the plan, when Germany were showing little sign of progress.

Their performance at Portugal 2004, indeed, fell far short of the nation's exacting standards. Drawn alongside Holland, Latvia and the Czech Republic, Germany were only denied a crucial opening round victory against the Dutch – perceived to be their biggest threats for top spot – by an 81st minute equaliser from future Hamburg forward Ruud van Nistelrooy. But the gleam of that 1-1 draw was scratched away massively by the following result, a goalless draw with European minnows Latvia – who were subsequently pummelled 3-0 by the Netherlands, and were participating in their first ever, and to date only, major international tournament.

Even that setback, though, hadn't ruled the Germans out. With two points from two games, victory over the Czechs, who rested most of their players having already qualified with two wins, would be enough for Germany to progress in second spot. It was a familiar scenario, that was to yield similar disappointment to the championships from four years earlier.

Inspirational midfielder Michael Ballack, who had been named man of the match in the opening two fixtures, gave the men in white a dream start, but a surprise collapse – again marked with a late goal, this time a winner from Milan Baros with just 13 minutes to play – sent the Germans packing, finishing third with just two points and two goals. The next day, popular boss Rudi Völler quit his position, stating: "I have the feeling that only someone who is untarnished and has a certain credibility – like I had four years ago – can do the job over the next two years."

It was a shocker, but the Germans had seen worse – the true 'disaster' that ignited a radical, national rethink had been the previously discussed European Championships in 2000. As Völler himself put it, in his departing statement: "This (Euro 2004) cannot be compared to the debacle four years ago."

*

The German squad might have lacked an untouchable leader figure in 2000 – although Ballack would go on to emerge as exactly that – with the Matthäus experiment clearly failing, but the DFB had a solution: appointing a legendary former player, Völler, as new national coach to succeed Ribbech within days of his departure. If the squad couldn't provide a sprinkling of stardust, at least the man on the bench would. Quite incredibly, it was Völler's first managerial role – he didn't even have the relevant coaching qualifications. And, though he left in the aftermath of a disappointing Euro 2004, he was still fondly received by supporters and players alike for a notable positive impact on the squad.

For Ballack, in particular, it was a welcome and familiar face at the time, given that Völler was part of the Leverkusen coaching set up where he had so thrived: "When Rudi Völler came in and took over as a coach, I was playing for Bayer Leverkusen, so I knew him and we had quite a good relationship, which helped after a really bad experience with Ribbeck and Stielike and the atmosphere in the team.

"It was important to install a coach who had the trust of the country, and a really good reputation. He was really close to most of the players, too, and there were a lot of Leverkusen players in the squad, so at least we had a good basis to play on.

"It was a tough job. On one side, you have to pay more attention to the youth, to bring youth players closer to the first team, but on the other side you still have to have a good national team to represent Germany for the next qualification, for 2002 and 2004.

"With a not much better squad, but a much better atmosphere, in 2002 we reached the World Cup final. That was the work from the coach – we know from that point what it means to be a team, what you can achieve as a team. We were not the best football team technically, we won three or four games 1-0, but we knew what our strengths were, what we could do, and what we couldn't.

"We achieved a really good result but still, in terms of football, technically, we weren't the best national team – when you see Spain or Brazil, they were playing much better football, beauty wise.

"But the most important thing was, in a close period, two years, to bring the fans back behind this national team, because we disappointed them very much in 2000."

Suddenly, the Germany squad were national heroes, and optimism was soaring again ahead of Euro 2004 – the 'blip' of 2000 well and truly consigned to the past. World Cup finalists, and the European team that progressed furthest, surely it wouldn't be unrealistic to expect them to go on and win the European Championships two years later? Not quite. More disappointment was in store in Portugal, as Germany crashed out at the group stage again.

While there was widespread disappointment, Nowotny took it particularly badly, labelling it worse than the previous European Championships, with familiar problems resurfacing: "For me, Euro 2004 was more of a disaster than Euro 2000. Our first game was against Holland, in something of a derby, and we drew but could have won, so it was an okay start. Nobody was panicking then.

"Then, we played Latvia and drew 0-0. That was when we went home, really. You could say that we lost the tournament in that draw. Of course, we could've won against the Czech Republic to go through, too, but lost there. As a more senior player by then, this was my 'disaster'. They had already qualified, so that was a big chance.

"But I don't think we went for it 100%, to risk everything. In this match, we only had in our mind what would happen if we lost. We weren't strong enough to beat them, because we only discussed with ourselves the negative things, not the positives.

"Because you can lose against the Czech Republic – you can lose against anyone – but you have to try everything. After the match, I felt that we didn't do enough to want to win the match.

"We have to be proud of being in the German national team, and show that we are strong enough. It was the players that were the problem, not the manager. Everybody was working on his own problems, but not the team problems. You can't have an offensive player standing at the front saying 'hey, good luck' to the defence. Everyone must help each other, but that didn't happen in Euro 2000 or 2004.

"Afterwards, everyone remembers Rudi Völler and what he said to the fans – he didn't know what more he could've done. And nor did the players – it was hard to understand why we had failed."

The surprisingly forgiving consensus amongst supporters was that Völler was doing his best with a mediocre group of players. For that reason, the disappointment didn't strike quite as painfully as in 2000 – but it extended Germany's generally poor tournament form since winning Euro 1996, with the prospects of that changing proving unlikely. But, for Ballack, there was a more positive conclusion to be drawn: this was part of a crucial learning curve for future successes.

"After reaching the 2002 final, we went out in the first round again in 2004, so there were some ups and downs. We weren't at a level where we could say 'Okay, we will go into this tournament and win it'. There were still some questions of this group before we went into the 2006 World Cup, in terms of quality of the squad, but that changed year after year.

"So, when all these young players came in, the generation just gone – Schweinsteiger, Lahm and Mertesacker – 2004 was their first involvement. But they needed that to grow. Then at the World Cup in 2006 they experienced the pressure and expectation of playing in front of your own crowd.

Chapter 2

"From there, 2008 they reached the final again, 2010 was a really good tournament, 2012 too, and 2014 they win. You could see more and more young players joined this national team, and it was much more stable because of the quality, which wasn't the case between 1998 and 2002."

But it wasn't just failure at an international tournament that Ballack credited with Germany's resurgence – otherwise England would surely have had a Spain-like spell of dominance or two since 1966 – it was another savvy managerial appointment, following Völler's resignation, that changed the complexion of the national team.

Truly, the realisation of their plan relied heavily upon the vision and philosophy of one man, who would rewrite Germany's footballing history in the space of just two, short years…

Chapter 3
The Jürgen Factor

Perhaps the biggest and boldest step the German footballing authorities took in their regeneration plans was to appoint Jürgen Klinsmann to his first managerial position, recalling him from the American wilderness – where he was playing amateur football pseudonymously, using the name Jay Göppingen, in the fourth-tier of US football at the time.

Following the popularity of Rudi Völler, and the promise displayed in the 2002 World Cup campaign – if not the 2004 Euros that followed – the DFB again turned to a high-profile former player who was relatively untried as a coach, appointing Klinsmann alongside the slightly more experienced assistant Joachim Löw, who had led Stuttgart to some success, and had managed in Austria and Turkey. The pair had met years earlier while taking their coaching badges, and discovered that they shared similar philosophies – a fateful meeting in the grander scheme of modern German football.

Speaking on the eve of Euro 2004, before his appointment, Klinsmann gave an idea of the perspective that would make him a candidate to revamp the ailing German side.

In an interview with *FourFourTwo* magazine, he said: "We have problems at the grass roots level because right now we are not developing as many creative players as we've had, like [Pierre] Littbarski or [Thomas] Hassler, in the recent generation.

"This comes down to an overall problem we have with the society because the kids have too many other things they can do. They're not playing football every day anymore – and if you're not playing in the backyard every day, you're not developing that amount of creativity like we would do.

"They have to find new ways of getting the kids back on the field and getting them playing more – and the more they play the better they get and the more creative they get. But there's a long way for

Germany to go to get the kids back to being enthusiastic about football."

Just weeks later – and almost before that interview had even hit the shelves – Klinsmann was appointed as the surprise successor to former strike-partner Rudi Völler.

His vision, one that the DFB clearly subscribed to, was key to the reimagining of German football – even though it was his assistant Joachim Löw that was at the helm for most of the progress.

It was a match made in heaven, from Michael Ballack's perspective. Reflecting on that pivotal appointment for this book, he said: "Klinsmann was the head coach. He had this idea, this picture of playing a different style of football – more offensive, more vertical, much quicker into the strikers. And you could see, and feel, from the first day that there was a plan – you could see a system, and a picture of how we would play. Klinsmann chose players for his system, and Jogi Löw was the coach that did a lot of work on the training pitch with the team."

As well as revamping the team's tactics and staffing structure – with another Germany icon and forward, Oliver Bierhoff, appointed General Manager to oversee Public Relations with the supporters – Klinsmann also made dramatic changes to the team's approach to national meet-ups and fixtures.

Ballack explained this contentious decision: "Klinsmann was living in America, and he brought in this more relaxed atmosphere around the national team. Before, we were always really well organised. So, when there was a game, we were meeting a week before in very quiet places to have the best preparation in terms of football, but not in terms of lifestyle.

"What Jürgen Klinsmann brought in was a more touchable national team for the country. So he went into big cities like Berlin and Hamburg, and we could go out before the game. He was more relaxed – younger players want to have a life outside of football. It was a big difference for the atmosphere; I could feel that.

"The players loved to go to the national team. Because it was not just two weeks of living in the middle of nowhere, eating, training, sleeping, repeat. That was the rhythm of the national team for over ten years.

"I know it's your profession, but also you have a life in between training sessions. So, you could go for a coffee, go out for an hour, have a little bit of free time, all these things were not really allowed before.

"Coaches would try to avoid the team from having contact with the outside world, so they could have the best preparation – but, sometimes, the opposite is the case. You should also find space outside of training and your work."

It's the sort of savvy, informed decision that almost comes as a surprise in football, a place where common sense rarely wins out. And it's an approach that would surely be welcomed by the England national team. At the 2010 World Cup in South Africa, captain John Terry and talisman Wayne Rooney both drew ire from supporters and the media when they complained of being 'bored' during the tournament. But, casting aside the churlish footballer stereotype, you can sympathise with the divisive duo; with the schoolmaster figure of Fabio Capello cracking the whip, and the squad stranded at a remote training base, it's not difficult to see how a group of young men would get a bit restless.

Terry allowed an insight into the dejected mood of the camp, in a controversially candid press conference during the tournament. He said: "We're in a hotel, we finish training and have lunch at one o'clock, but then we have hours to spare. There are things to do around the training camp: mini darts tournaments, snooker and pool. But a bit of boredom kicks in. It's six or seven hours until we meet up for dinner again."

That might sound tolerable, and even therapeutic for a day or two, but not weeks on end. Capello dictated when and how the players trained and ate, and banned the players' families, in what must have felt like something of a boot camp, rather than a once-in-a-lifetime opportunity. It was removing this exact kind of vibe that really refreshed and reinvigorated the German squad, Ballack says.

"That was something Jürgen Klinsmann brought in from America. And this helped the team to have a new picture of the national team, to motivate players. Come on, it's a fantastic thing to play for your national team, and be part of a good community, represent your country and have contact with the fans.

31

"It's a small thing, but important. When you train for the whole year with your club, and then go to the national team, you need that bit of life in-between. Klinsmann got a lot of criticism from the media for that, but he had his picture and what I liked was that he didn't care about what comes from outside. And the plan worked – we played a good World Cup.

"When he stepped back, Jogi Löw took over. Because he was next to Klinsmann, he could follow the same idea, and improve with the squad he had. From there, the national team grew."

*

Writing for the BBC during the South Africa World Cup in 2010, Klinsmann offered fascinating insight into how that rebuilding process began. And, straight from the off, he was given the freedom to make a major shift in the set-up: "I got the chance to decide on the direction we took when I agreed to take over as Germany coach that summer, with current manager Joachim Löw as my assistant.

"'Jogi' and I began the whole regeneration process by trying to give our national team an identity. When Jogi and I took over the German side, we made our plans very public and made it clear that we were trying to rebuild from the bottom up.

"The German Football Association (DFB) helped us by putting a lot of pressure on all the first and second division teams in the Bundesliga to build academy programmes and ensure talented young players were coming through but we still had to decide on our playing style.

"To do that, we quizzed everyone we could. We held workshops with German coaches and players, asking them to write down on flip charts three things: how they wanted to play, how they wanted to be seen to be playing by the rest of the world and how the German public wanted to see us playing.

"If we could define all of that, we thought we could lay out how we wanted to work and then, from there, sort out the training and paperwork behind the scenes.

"What we ended up with amounted to 10 or 12 bullet points laying out our proposals. We then announced that it was our intention to play a fast-paced game, an attacking game and a proactive game.

"That last term was something the Germans did not really like because they did not really understand what proactive meant. We just told them it meant we did not react to what our opponents did, we played the way that was right for us.

"Once we had done all that, we created a curriculum for German football and presented it to the Bundesliga and DFB boards. At that point, I told them I did not have the time to implement the strategy at all levels because I only had two years to prepare for the World Cup, so I asked for Germany's Under-21 team to adopt it and that was it.

"I brought in a former international team-mate of mine, Dieter Eilts, to run the under-21s and said they had to play the same way as the senior team because they would be a feeder for it."

Though Klinsmann's focus was very much to look forward, with the regeneration of Germany his priority, he was also responsible for ensuring that his side didn't let themselves down when the world's greatest tournament was being held on home turf – yes, target the future, but make sure you address 2006, too.

And, because of that, it wasn't always smooth sailing for the manager, with pre-tournament anxiety and mixed results combining to put Klinsmann under some pressure. In fact, it would've been no surprise had he been relieved of his duties at one point – but one pivotal result turned that around, and the rest is actual history.

"I was always looking long-term but I knew our plans would be measured by our success at the 2006 World Cup. There was a lot of negative media at the start. Everybody agreed German football had to change after 2004 but nobody actually wanted to adopt our proposals.

"For example, we told the Bundesliga teams and coaches that their players needed to be fitter to play the kind of football we wanted to play.

"That meant carrying out fitness tests every three months, which did not go down well with some clubs because I was able to prove that some of them were training their players properly and others were not. I was basically doubted for the two years I was coach - and when we lost 4-1 to Italy in a friendly game three months before the 2006 World Cup, everybody wanted my blood!

"We had another game three weeks later against the United States and we won that one 4-1. That victory saved my job and kept me in charge for the World Cup because the DFB had been ready to make a change. They wanted the conservative approach again, not the revolution.

"But I kept on being positive, explaining that this was how I wanted us to play. I did not know if we would master it in time for the 2006 World Cup but we would give it a shot."

Despite the DFB's doubts, that USA result – Klinsmann enjoying a 'Mark Robins moment' akin to Sir Alex Ferguson's career saving FA Cup victory at Manchester United in 1990 – meant that they got fully behind their manager. And everything he asked was granted, which was soon reflected in the way his players responded to his instructions.

"We had the players for four solid weeks before the tournament began and were able to get our thoughts across. They agreed to train the way we wanted them to and do extra work. Soon they started to believe in the system.

"That was crucial because, no matter what your job is, you need to identify yourself with the work that you are doing and be happy. I was happy because, as a former striker, I liked the style we intended to play. I could never coach a team that played defensive-minded football.

"I also think the players understood that I was the one taking the risk and that if it did not work out the DFB would send me packing back to California. We started well at the 2006 World Cup and the public began to feel that something special was going to happen.

"In the second game, when we beat Poland with a last-minute goal, the whole nation embraced us and said: 'Yeah, that's our team and that's how we want them to play'. We lost in the semi-final against Italy but I was still very proud."

Despite that success, Klinsmann chose to walk away from his position – just as he'd won the public over. He doesn't express any regret over that decision, given what followed – he might not be able to polish a 2014 World Cup winner's medal, but he certainly set Germany on the right path to lifting the famous trophy. And perhaps his most decisive contribution was anointing his successor.

"After that World Cup, I was burned out after two years of banging my head against a wall but I made it clear to the DFB that Jogi had to take over after me to continue the job we had started.

"He has continued to develop that initial style of play and is enjoying success. It has taken Germany six years to learn to play it properly - and it has developed along the way - but the players are completely comfortable with it now.

"Germany's style of play might work for England because, in a way, Germany now play a lot like a typical Premier League team, with the emphasis on pacey attacks."

*

That Klinsmann now is making a similar impression on the United States national team is testament to his philosophies and coaching methods. But the former Tottenham striker shouldn't take all the glory – indeed, it was his successor and former assistant, Löw, that took their masterplan to the next level; blooding and trusting the core of the 2014 World Cup winning side, in a sensational and brave period of management...

Chapter 4
Jung, Löw:
How Germany learned that you can win things with kids

Would it be too optimistic to try to associate England and the Premier League with Germany's success in 2014 – to steal some of the vast credit lavished upon the Bundesliga? Almost certainly, but two of the World Cup winning squad were *technically* products of British youth systems, and qualify as 'homegrown' in England.

They are defender Shkordran Mustafi, who spent three years at Everton as a teenager, after joining the Toffees from the Hamburg youth system; and third-choice goalkeeper Ron-Robert Zieler, a Manchester United reserve team player for five years after being snapped up as a 16-year-old from FC Cologne.

That neither still plays in the Premier League – Mustafi left for Sampdoria before joining Valencia in the aftermath of the World Cup, and Zieler returned to Germany in 2010 with Hannover – says much about the competition's opportunities for young players. The extent of Mustafi's first team action at Goodison was a 15-minute substitute appearance in the Europa League, before being allowed to leave on a free transfer as a 'money raising' exercise by David Moyes.

Zieler, meanwhile, did not make a competitive appearance for Manchester United; the closest he came was sitting on the bench for a League Cup match – though the promising keeper did win the Manchester Senior Cup twice with the Under-18 side.

He enjoyed further junior success with the German Under-19 team that won the 2008 European Championships, for whom he was first choice, but that was only rewarded with a short-term loan stint at

Chapter 4

Northampton Town in League One the following season, where he made two appearances. For Zieler, highly rated in his homeland, it was probably the final straw – and a return to the Bundesliga beckoned, along with genuine first team opportunities.

Reflecting on his time in England, Zieler clearly holds no grudges for how his spell at Old Trafford turned out. His move to Manchester was always going to be an 'educational' trip, a platform, rather than somewhere he was going to establish himself.

He said: "I started at Cologne at the age of ten, where I began my goalkeeper training. At 14, I got into the youth national team – you're only young, and right at the beginning of your career, but you start to learn how to be professional. They start to prepare you for the first team, for Germany, straight away. The big focus is the professional attitude, that's taught from an early age.

"Going to Manchester United at 16, obviously I knew that it was going to be really hard to become a first team player. Back then it was Edwin van der Sar who was in goal, so the possibility of me taking that space was very small.

"But I was thinking, to play for such a big club, it was going to be a good development – learning was the most important thing. Training with van der Sar and Ben Foster, learning from them and from top goalkeeping coaches. This is why I went to Manchester.

"After four or five years, I knew I had to move on. They were looking for someone else for the first team, but they wanted someone more experienced. It was difficult for any of the young players to get a chance. A few – like Danny Welbeck, Tom Cleverley and Jonny Evans – did, but most of us moved on to other clubs."

Zieler's departure was back to his homeland, with Hannover, after a successful end of season trial period. Joining in July 2010, as a 21-year-old, he did enough to earn a starting berth by the following January, and has remained first choice ever since. In August 2011, barely a year after returning to the Bundesliga, he was handed his first full international call-up – making his debut three months later, the 50th player to do so under Joachim Löw's tutelage. The next summer, within two years of leaving United unwanted, he was part of Germany's Euro 2012 squad.

Clearly, his decision to go home paid off: "At that time, and for maybe ten years before, Germany was struggling with the league, so the clubs gave young players the opportunity to play. Most of the Bundesliga clubs couldn't afford to spend as much as the English teams – even the ones playing for relegation there spend tens of millions on big players. But in Germany that was not possible.

"Good young players were given the opportunity to play in the first team a bit earlier, and it worked out. Like you see at Borussia Dortmund, they were struggling, and then suddenly they give youth players like Götze and Schmelzer an opportunity, even in Europe.

"So my move to Hannover, of course, was motivated by first team opportunities. Maybe I should've made the step a year or two earlier. I spoke with my goalkeeping coach, Eric Steele, back then and he was thinking the same – they were saying that my time at Manchester United was over more or less, and that it was better for me to move on.

"I had a coach at Hannover who was looking for performance. I trained well and played well for the reserve team, and he gave me the opportunity to play in the Bundesliga. In the end, I made the right decision to go back to Germany – in Manchester, that would not have been possible for me."

And, ominously for everyone outside of Germany, Zieler doesn't think the youth culture is going away any time soon. He said: "At the moment, the youth system in Germany seems to be really good, and we have a lot of young players coming through again – we won the Under-19s European Championship, we won the Under-21s a few years ago. So we have a lot of fantastic young players, which is the work of the Bundesliga clubs in the early stages."

Something that is a recurring theme throughout the interviews with Bundesliga or Germany players and staff for this book is a wariness of complacency – a desire to keep pushing for further development and success.

One of those at the forefront of this mission is Pellegrino Matarazzo, the American manager of FC Nurnberg's Under-19 team, formerly a lower league journeyman in Germany, plying his trade mostly in the third tier. His coaching career promises to be more auspicious, already establishing himself as one to watch, barely five years after retirement.

So what is the key to his success, and that of the Bundesliga generally?

"German football has a very detailed approach to young players, and we have a detailed curriculum at this club. In Germany, it is a holistic approach to coaching – in Spain it is very technical, in Italy it's tactical, in the UK and US it is physical. But, in Germany, it is thought through, and has a very good balance across those things.

"In the Nurnberg curriculum, we have learning objectives, a vision of what players should be able to do when they leave our academy. Those are broken down throughout age groups – some are technical, tactical, physical, etc., all age appropriate.

"It's about developing our players to come to our first team. We orientate ourselves to what we need, which is players who can jump into the first team – but it's a broad list, there are many things they need to be able to do.

"So, for example, technically they need to be good on the ball, passing, dribbling, shooting, heading offensively and defensively. We have a list of qualities for each category that reflects how we want to play football."

If that all sounds pretty par for the course, and what you'd imagine, there is a striking difference between the English and German approaches to youth football – Matarazzo reveals that winning isn't always the be all and end all for his side.

"At youth, our approach is learning how to win, and success in our actions and one-on-ones. It's not always about the end result, but each individual battle being successful. A defeat doesn't mean failure or a bad performance.

"Obviously, the older they get, the more emphasis players have on the result. And the younger boys do have expectations – we hope to see certain things in their development, and it is assessed in terms of what needs to be learned – but not always in terms of the result."

For Matarazzo, the development of a young player isn't as simple as winning games – he is pioneering a tailored coaching style that is geared around a player's needs, rather than a standard procedure.

"The emphasis and direction of German youth coaching is individualisation. At Elite schools, we produce strength and weakness profiles for each player, and the coaches can work according to these individual objectives, whether they're athletic or tactical.

"So if players A, L, and Z have weaknesses with their defensive heading, they'll work together in smaller groups for four to six weeks, before we analyse whether they've improved, and need to move on to something else."

I'm speaking to him at the end of the season, where Nurnberg's Under-19's have just finished a post-season tournament, the 2015 Volksbank Cup in Nienburg – some 500 kilometres away from Nuremberg, despite the similarity in spelling.

There, Matarazzo had been afforded first-hand glimpses of talent from both England and Spain – as his side lined up against Tottenham, Liverpool, and Malaga. Against the might of those outfits, his team were relative minnows, but still managed to reach the final – where they were only beaten by Liverpool on penalties, 7-6. Not bad for a second division club's Under-19 team. For the coach, it was another sign of German youth football's stature.

He said: "We actually expected the competition to be a bit stronger. We finished 7th in the South/South-West Under-19s Bundesliga, and have a decent side, but thought we'd have tougher ties.

"You could see that Malaga were very technical, but not direct enough – they'd do things where you'd immediately tell the boys to play with more risk in Germany. And Tottenham were very British, physical, quick and strong. But Liverpool were more technical than we'd expected."

*

Bullish confidence and faith in youth stems from the very top of the German game – national team manager Joachim Löw really took predecessor Jürgen Klinsmann's plans for a fresh start and ran with them.

His decision to turn to the youth, though, wasn't as revolutionary as it might have seemed at the time. At the UEFA Under-21 Championships in 2009, Germany won their first ever title at that level, indicating that a new breed of stars was ready to step up after excelling in Sweden.

They claimed the crown in style, demolishing Stuart Pearce's England 4-0 in the final, with a skinny 20-year-old playmaker running riot – Mesut Özil at the heart of things in a stark forewarning of what was to come barely a year later when the senior sides of the two countries met at the 2010 World Cup.

Özil, on the back of his breakthrough season at Werder Bremen, set up Gonzalo Castro for the opener, before doubling Germany's advantage with a long-range free kick, and then releasing Sandro Wagner for a third – the former Bayern Munich youth player then adding a fourth.

Despite his two-goal haul in the final, Wagner is one of just a handful of players from that line-up who haven't gone on to become household names across the globe. Germany's starting XI that day in Malmo included future World Cup winners Manuel Neuer, Jérôme Boateng, Benedikt Höwedes, Mats Hummels, Sami Khedira, and Özil.

By contrast, the teamsheet of their English opposition read: Scott Loach; Martin Cranie, Micah Richards, Nedum Onuoha, Kieran Gibbs; Fabrice Muamba, Lee Cattermole, Mark Noble, James Milner, Adam Johnson; Theo Walcott. Only Milner has gone on to even play in a World Cup.

In fact, while Özil was tearing England apart in South Africa, alongside three others from that Germany Under-21 line up – Neuer, Boateng, and Khedira – Milner was the sole England player to make the same step up from the Under-21s.

Of the German line-up, only goal-scorer Wagner has failed to go on to be a senior international – though teammates Sebastian Boenisch and Fabian Johnson opted to represent Poland and the USA respectively instead.

The phrase 'golden generation' has negative connotations in England, but Germany's was truly emerging – it completed a remarkable hat-trick of youth level success, adding to the Under-19 and Under-17 European titles lifted less than a year earlier.

The successful Under-19s line-up included the Bender twins Lars and Sven, while the star man for the Under-17s in 2009 was a certain Mario Götze, named the tournament's Best Player aged just 16. He was given his full debut the next year. Subsequent German Under-17 sides reached the final in Euro 2011, 2012 and 2015, while their Under-19 contingent were victorious at Euro 2014.

So when Löw announced his squad for the 2010 World Cup, it probably shouldn't have been a surprise that its average age, 24, was the joint-lowest for the tournament – with Ghana and North Korea.

But, however galling that 4-1 Round of 16 defeat was for England, it wasn't this German generation's defining result; that was to come four years later, in another rampant victory – the unforgettable 7-1 humiliation of Brazil in the 2014 semi-final. There, six of the players that lined up for the 2009 Under-21 final started, as Germany confirmed their status as best team in the world in some style.

Such international achievement has reinforced the domestic focus on youth development, making for a self-serving cycle of success. In 2014, German clubs spent more than €120million on their academies, with the total amount invested into future talents since 2002 topping €1billion.

And this doesn't just make the Bundesliga a breeding ground for youngsters, a mere testing ground for Germany – one of the benefits of the academy policy is clubs becoming increasingly 'self-sufficient' in terms of playing staff. In 2000, just six per cent of the players in the league were under-23. Within a decade, that had risen to 15%. This value for money means that, when sides do have to spend money and sign someone, there's more available in the coffers, allowing for better acquisitions.

The DFB itself has 21 district and five regional training centres on top of the league's academies and ever increasing and expanding youth set-ups. Domestically, the plan has come to fruition as well as it has internationally. For example, during the 2013 Champions League, when the final was an all-German affair between Bayern and Dortmund, a whopping 26 of the players the two teams named in their UEFA squads that season were homegrown and eligible to play for Germany. More than half of them came through the talent development programme introduced by the DFB in 2003.

That scheme was charged with spotting future stars between the ages of eight and 14, and fast-tracking their development, picking from a vast talent pool covering 366 areas of the country; it was staffed by more than 1,000 part-time UEFA B license holding coaches, who both scout and train players. As Robin Dutt, Sporting Director of the German FA puts it: "We have 80 million people in Germany and, I think, before 2000, nobody noticed a lot of talent. Now we notice everyone."

*

If Özil's emergence as a first team mainstay was an obvious progression for a sublime young talent, another player's promotion was borne more out of circumstance – the shock and tragic suicide of Robert Enke in November 2009 left a space between the sticks for the 2010 World Cup. Rene Adler was the man to step up, with Manuel Neuer his deputy, but a pre-tournament injury to the new number one meant that Neuer had been catapulted into first choice from third in a matter of months.

That wasn't the only injury to hamper and totally alter Löw's plans for South Africa. Main man Michael Ballack and regular deputies Heiko Westermann and Simon Rolfes were all ruled out, leaving a huge hole in the middle of the park. It was a seemingly disastrous turn of events for a World Cup year. Indeed, Ballack's injury in the English FA Cup final, a result of a reckless challenge from young compatriot Kevin-Prince Boateng, was met with public uproar, and confirmed Boateng's role as public enemy number one – not helped by Boateng's decision to change international allegiance to Ghana instead, and play against Germany at the tournament.

But Löw had a solution – in a friendly against Argentina, three months before the tournament, he had experimented with Schweinsteiger as a holding midfielder, rather than his usual left wing position, which he'd lost to Lukas Podolski, deploying him alongside Ballack for the first time. Clearly, despite tepid reviews at the time, Löw liked what he saw, as the Bayern Munich man stepped into

Ballack's almighty boots, partnering Sami Khedira at the World Cup, another player fast-tracked from the Under-21s side.

That Schweinsteiger tweak left a gap in the squad for another winger and, in the same friendly, Löw handed Thomas Müller his first start on the right flank – a position he would come to redefine, even producing his own name for it, *Raumdeuter*, or 'space investigator'. When Müller was substituted in the 1-0 loss, he was replaced by debutant Toni Kroos, another whose position in the squad would be upgraded massively by the time of the World Cup as a result of Germany's 'injury crisis'.

It meant that Joachim Löw picked Germany's youngest World Cup squad in 76 years, and that youthful exuberance and fearlessness took the tournament by surprise – England weren't the only opponents blown away, as Argentina were dismantled 4-0 in the following round, with Schweinsteiger particularly excelling in his new role, setting up two goals while man marking Lionel Messi out of the game. This was a matured, almost unrecognisable, player to the exciting 21-year-old winger that had almost bagged a hat-trick – denied only by a free kick being cruelly credited as an own goal rather than awarded to him – in the 2006 World Cup third place playoff.

The success of Schweinsteiger's switch, which was later mirrored at Bayern, also paved the way for future adjustments – Phillip Lahm's deployment in the centre of midfield during the 2014 campaign, for instance.

Buoyed by their third place finish in South Africa, Löw continued to experiment, clearly enjoying his tinkering. In a November friendly after the tournament, against Sweden, he handed debuts to Mario Götze, then 18, Andre Schürrle, and Lewis Holtby. There were run outs, too, for various other youngsters, including Mats Hummels, Marko Marin, Marcel Schmelzer, Kevin Grosskreutz, and Andreas Beck. Like the seemingly pivotal pre-World Cup friendly with Argentina, the result in Gothenburg wasn't much to shout about – playing out a goalless draw – but the performance, and the potential, certainly was.

And it wasn't just young players he was developing, he was also fostering a new team ethos. International duty with Löw wasn't to be a daunting, stuffy experience steeped in traditional behaviour and approaches, rather he wanted to generate a club-style atmosphere. To this end, his focus shifted from the temporary to the long-term – preferring to pick his squads based on their potential rather than their hype as flavour of the month. If you were having a tough time at club level, you wouldn't immediately have to start panicking about your international place too to compound your misery.

In many ways, it was a reminder of one of the changes the DFB introduced on the back of the Euro 2000 disaster – announcing the creation of a new national 'B' team, Team 2006, specifically with the intention of trying out and developing players for the home World Cup, to ensure similar humiliation wouldn't happen on home soil. Away from the glare of official fixtures, this outfit was used experimentally, and to some success – with many players trialled in Team 2006 matches going on to become full internationals. Although the team was dismantled after the tournament it was established for, Löw has since adopted a similar approach to friendly games. A more effective use than the meaningless and pointless non-events held by many sides, often solely for the appearance fee offered by the host stadium.

Handing Götze his debut after the 2010 World Cup, for instance, made the prodigy Germany's fourth youngest international of all time. Two more of Löw's debutants make it into the top ten – Max Meyer is sixth after appearing against Poland in a pre-World Cup friendly in 2014, Julian Draxler seventh after taking part in a Euro 2012 warm-up versus Switzerland. All three were part of the squad crowned world champions in Brazil. Four other teenagers have been handed international debuts by Löw – Gonzalo Castro, Marko Marin, Leon Goretzka and Maximilian Arnold – meaning that of the 27 Germans to make their international bow in their teens, seven have been selected by him, more than any of his predecessors. Klinsmann, by comparison, introduced just one teen – defender Lukas Sinkiewicz in 2005, who now plies his trade in the German third division.

*

When he's not coaching the national team – in the long periods when Bundesliga action takes priority, and international managers are left kicking their heels somewhat – Joachim Löw clearly pays close attention to the development of his squad, and future additions. In 2011, he visited the Freiburg academy, the club for whom he is record goal scorer after three stints during his playing days, and spoke clearly and directly to the talents there about what he expected.

Explaining his tactical philosophy, he said: "The space on the pitch has become smaller, the time to act scarce. Individual skill is therefore the most important factor in training, more important than the system.

"We need to make the simple into the very special; the passing game, the timing, the pressing and trapping, the game without the ball, how we deal with one-on-one situations, how we quickly find solutions in small spaces."

It is a rare and intriguing insight into exactly what up-and-coming German players were being taught ahead of their successful World Cup winning campaign. It contrasts with the English approach, which still centres on physicality. In a recent advert for a place at the Sheffield Wednesday academy online, for example, the listing specified minimum height requirements for would be goalkeeper applicants. It included demands for players wanting to join the Under-16 team to be at least 6'1", even though many boys won't go through their final growth spurt until their late teens.

Such short-sightedness, though, doesn't extend to Löw, the surprise coaching visionary, who never quite became a success at club level, but who has been able to take the national team on substantially. He enjoyed the greatest ever start for a Germany manager, with five consecutive victories – leading them to top of the FIFA rankings in July 2014 for the first time in 20 years.

Key to that success has been his ability to mostly avoid the reactionary nature of top level football, as evidenced by the way he stepped in to defend Mario Götze towards the end of the 2014/15 season, having failed to live up to his World Cup winning goal the previous summer – with even Bayern Munich's honorary President Franz Beckenbauer amongst the starlet's critics.

Speaking out in favour of the player he handed an international debut to, Löw said: "I don't understand the partially unobjective discussion and criticism. That's how it's like in our business. Not long ago,

Mario was the best Götze of all time, our World Cup hero – and now everything's bad. That's just too easy.

"It's not fair to measure Mario against his goal in the World Cup final, nobody can live up to those expectations. One thing is clear to me – Mario is an exceptionally skilled player, a player who can make the difference.

"He is also allowed to make mistakes. Mario has a great future at FC Bayern, and certainly in the national team too. He is without doubt one of the best footballers in the world."

It's not hard to see why players warm to Löw, and how he has motivated the Germany squad to utilise its fullest potential. But there's plenty of tactical thinking that goes into Löw's preparations for fixtures, too; with an emphasis on the collective rather than just the individual. Speaking to *World Soccer Magazine* after the 2014 World Cup, he explained exactly how he approached the tournament in terms of squad selection.

"Players who are team-orientated, who integrate well and are communicative. Those who want to take on responsibility, are disciplined and ambitious. For every game, I wanted everyone on the bench to be ready for action. I also wanted to take young players who could put pressure on the more senior guys and would handle themselves positively in the group – for example, Erik Durm and Matthias Ginter. In January we'd whittled it down to 30 outfield players."

He also revealed a slight difference in his approach to predecessor Jürgen Klinsmann – who liked to adopt a fully relaxed national team atmosphere. Löw, instead, likes to keep his players guessing: "I've always worked on a case-by-case basis, deciding whether to keep the guys in full concentration or letting them off the leash a little. Striking the balance between tension and relaxation is vital in a tournament."

So what next for the Bundestrainer and his young band of world champions? What challenges face Germany after the 2014 World Cup? "In certain areas we have to begin again. Opponents will have analysed the way we play and because of that we will have to come up with new methods. We are on top of the world, but the trick is to stay there, to become even better."

In many ways, that quote could be applied to the process German football as a whole has applied over the last few years. Not only has that reaped benefits on the pitch, but off-field the Bundesliga has become one of the world's best run divisions, and a global franchise fit to rival the Premier League…

Chapter 5
Debt prevention rules, OK? The original Financial Fair Play

German football is just as traditional as the English game – with leading clubs rooted in their histories. Histories which help define the way such clubs are run. Originally, they were established as generic sports clubs – initially for gymnastics, before other sporting endeavours were added. They were public organisations, not-for-profit multi-sport associations, run by and for their members. Bayern Munich wasn't set up to become a global brand and company, it was established for the health and fitness of the local community. Indeed, German football teams were prohibited from being 'businesses' until as recently as 2000, and many still aren't – Dortmund remain the only publicly listed company in the Bundesliga.

At the turn of the millennium, a period of modernisation took place, when the old-fashioned set ups were brought up to date, with the pro football divisions turned into limited companies. CEOs, in turn, replaced presidents at the top of the hierarchy. These changes were all geared towards attracting investment and investors, by adopting what was perceived as a more professional structure. But it wasn't Russian oligarchs like Roman Abramovich – who bought Chelsea in 2003 – they were trying to appeal to, as the Bundesliga created some savvy restrictions.

Chief among them was the rule that was established to prevent takeovers – known as the 50+1 rule. It stipulates that the club itself must retain at least 50 per cent of the shares, plus one share, to ensure that the team's members would always be the majority shareholders. This rule means that no outside investor, however rich or enthusiastic, can own more than 49.9 per cent of a Bundesliga club. This law means that clubs are a cooperative, rather than following a benefactor model, and reinforces their link to the local community. Companies and wealthy individuals can buy a stake, but the relationship is much more of a partnership than a plaything.

The rule was introduced in 2001, when the two divisions of the Bundesliga broke away from the DFB to secure better commercial contracts – an echo of the Premier League's formation almost 20 years previously. The DFB, like the English FA, continues to be responsible for lower levels of football and, in December 2012, that amounted to nearly 7 million players across 175,000 teams in 25,650 registered clubs – receiving three per cent of TV income and two per cent of ticket sales from the Bundesliga to help fund grassroots training and development.

When the 50+1 rule was implemented, it was initially perceived to be restrictive on the potential of German clubs. They feared they'd be less favourable propositions than their English counterparts, as a potential ego-booster for a billionaire – which is almost certainly true: these filthy rich owners want to do everything their own way, not be held accountable by a board and members.

Martin Kind, president of Hannover, challenged the ruling in 2011, saying: "The rule means the loss of many Bundesliga clubs' ability to compete nationally and internationally. And, in some ways, it prevents further development of German football, especially those clubs that play in the lower half of the Bundesliga as they do not have enough financial resources. The ownership rule should be abandoned or modified." But, when it went to a vote, 32 of the 36 clubs in the top two Bundesliga divisions went against him. Clearly, the desire to sell out is in the extreme minority in Germany.

A reason that club dissonance is so rare is because, while clubs miss out on billionaire takeovers, none would be burdened by the huge levels of debt that clubs like Manchester United have shouldered following the Glazer family takeover in 2003. In turn, none would have their history rewritten like Hull City are currently battling owner Assem Allam to avoid.

The sanctity of the 50+1 rule was reinforced barely a year after its creation, when German football had its own 'ITV Digital' moment – with the collapse of the pay-TV broadcaster Kirch Group in 2002, the organisation that owned Bundesliga rights at the time. Christian Seifert, Bundesliga CEO, reflected: "When Kirch filed for bankruptcy, it was a real economic shock to the league. After the Bosman ruling, the Bundesliga had a high proportion of older, overseas players, and the clubs had wages to pay, liabilities from investing in their stadiums. The difficulties they had were a wake up – they realised they had to be more careful with the finances."

This also coincided with the fall-out from the 'disaster tournament' and the subsequent 10-year plan: "The youth academies were introduced at around the same time and the clubs saw it made sense to bring through good young players, financially as well as in football terms." All in, the clubs subscribed wholeheartedly to the league's plan – and the community ownership element was far from some airy-fairy idea. The club's members hold genuine power, as they elect officials – including those at the very top. Everyone is accountable, and can be held responsible, so reckless short-termism is generally ill advised for those in senior roles. Otherwise, they'll soon find themselves departing.

Of the top two divisions in Germany, only two clubs aren't owned or controlled by their members – the exceptions being works teams Wolfsburg and Leverkusen, owned by Volkswagen and chemical company Bayer respectively. Each have developed strong roots in their working class areas, having been founded by factory workers, and are therefore considered compliant in many ways anyway.

Christian Seifert explains: "If a company is supporting football in a club for more than 20 years, then it can acquire the majority. The idea is that a company has by then proved to fans and the league that they take their engagement in the Bundesliga seriously – that it's not just a fancy toy or part-time cash injection that [could] change from one day to another." And that judgment is clearly correct – under Volkswagen's guidance, Wolfsburg won the first title in their history in 2009 and continue to be a major force in the Bundesliga.

A third team, Hoffenheim, have a slightly different set-up – after climbing the ranks from amateur football with the financial backing of a local billionaire. Though tycoon Dietmar Hopp owns 96% of the club's shares, they still conform to the Bundesliga ruling as he has just 49% of the voting rights. And Hoffenheim's rise very much makes them outsiders in German football with the reaction to their success comparable to the naysayers of Chelsea and Manchester City's recent achievements, but arguably to a greater extent, as they were in the fifth division when Hopp took charge. But even he plays by the rules – and, no matter how responsible his riches might have been for their successes, the club isn't entirely reliant on him, or completely under his control.

Having learned from the mistakes of the Premier League, the Bundesliga clubs are staunch believers in the 50+1 ruling – Hans-Joachim Watzke, CEO at Dortmund, included. He told *FourFourTwo* magazine, when discussing the issue: "In the long run, it's the better solution. Whenever you have investors, some kind of corporate demeanour begins to engulf the club, and that's not our mentality.

"The German fan wants to have the feeling that he is part of the whole. In England, the fan is now basically a customer and can, by and large, live with that. But if you tell a German supporter that he is just a customer, he's going to kill you. He has to feel connected to the club and that's only possible through the 50+1 rule, because when you really get down to it, the parent club's members are still in control.

"Of course, we run the limited company autonomously, but if the members one day think I should leave, they can sack me."

It is one of a number of decisions taken that have left Bundesliga clubs out of pocket when compared to English clubs, but for the 'right' reasons. Christian Seifert continues with the theme in greater detail.

"Munich makes €30 to €40million less a year in ticket prices than Manchester United – over ten years that is [more than] €300million. The league has no power to interfere with this, the clubs decide on their own. But some kind of common sense prevails.

"But it's very hard for the clubs. Every year in the magazines you see double pages about how much are the prices of tickets, and bratwurst, and beer and everyone gets in a s***storm if the price of bratwurst goes up by ten per cent."

But would Bayern and Co adopt the Premier League model in the future, if they could get away with it?

"You cannot tell but, from today's perspective, the clubs would not change the strategy. It would not be accepted. For the Yellow Wall,

[Dortmund] could easily charge double the price, but they choose to have a price the lower social classes can afford.

"They could also sell 90 per cent of their tickets as season tickets, but they choose not to. They like to give as many people as possible the chance to go to matches – we see the Bundesliga as an important part of society.

"We have a holistic approach, based on the financial, the game, and society. If we don't have success in all three dimensions, we don't consider it a success at all."

And it's not just big talk – Dortmund really could hike up the price for a spot amid the Südtribüne – their terrace for standing supporters – and still fill out their stadium. When they reached the 2013 Champions League final, BVB were allocated 24,042 Wembley seats for their supporters, and received more than half a million applications for them. The demand is certainly there.

Yet, at home games, many of Dortmund's 55,000 season ticket holders have paid an average of just £9 to attend – no wonder they're so passionate in support. Arsenal, despite having an attendance that is 20,000 lower, make considerably more on match-day than Dortmund do. Not that the German side feel like the ones missing out.

Marketing director Carsten Cramer explained to the *BBC*: "Why are tickets cheap? Football is part of people's lives and we want to open the doors for all of society. We need the people, they spend their hearts, their emotions with us – they are the club's most important asset.

"What is the economic sense for the club to increase the price by ten cent? For the overall economic success of the club, it is not important to increase the price of a litre of a beer. It is still money, but not a lot to the club – but it does affect our fans if they are spending their money match after match.

"We try to be as fair as possible – it is easier to ask sponsors for cash than the fans. [Arsenal's match day revenue] is impressive. But if we were to ask for prices like this, we would lose the people.

"We are a football club. If the football doesn't run properly, the rest of the business would not work. The business is part of a train, but not the engine."

Similarly, Dortmund were encouraged by Puma, the club's shirt manufacturer, to increase the RRP of a replica shirt, having previously sold it at the same price for three years. A Premier League club wouldn't need telling twice, you'd feel – Dortmund, though, refused.

And there's another reason that teams throughout the Bundesliga generally don't follow the massively corporate focus at Arsenal, or even the investment models at Chelsea and Man City – because they wouldn't make enough of a difference. That's because the predominant cause of the gulf between the divisions is the incredible riches on offer to Premier League sides through their television deal.

While Bayern are the top earners through the Bundesliga's deal, making around €36.9million in the 2013/14 season, with Dortmund not far behind on €35.5million, those figures are comprehensively dwarfed by their English equivalents.

In fact, of the list of highest TV deal incomes in Europe, eight out of ten are from the Premier League. Only joint-first Real Madrid and Barcelona, and ninth placed Juventus, prevent an English lockout. A combination of a new, more fairly distributed deal in Spain, and a huge new Premier League package beginning in 2016, however, means that will soon change.

Manchester United, who are seventh in the list – as they were in the Premier League despite a nightmare season – received €106.9million in domestic TV money: more than Bayern, Dortmund and Leverkusen combined. At the end of the 2016/17 season, the side that finishes bottom of the Premier League tablet will receive around €140million in television prize money, under the terms of the new £5.1billion deal. It means Bayern will be earning around a third of what the Premier League's worst club does in television rights.

The winners of the Premier League will bank close to €210million in prize money, a fifty per cent increase on Real and Barca's current plush deal – which will soon plummet in value. In the 2013/14 campaign, the duopoly of La Liga were enjoying a disproportionate share of the television money – third biggest Valencia received just €48million, while the smallest cut was €18million for Almeira.

By the time of the new Premier League deal – the biggest in world sport barring the NFL's – those giants will be cut down to size, but still banking far more than Bayern and Dortmund.

Top ten recipients of TV money in Europe, 2013/14

Rank	Team	Nation	Amount
1	Real Madrid/Barcelona	Spain	€140million
2	Liverpool	England	€117million
3	Man City	England	€115.8million
4	Chelsea	England	€112.9million
5	Arsenal	England	€111.4million
6	Tottenham	England	€107.6million
7	Man United	England	€106.9million
8	Everton	England	€102million
9	Juventus	Italy	€94million
10	Newcastle	England	€92.8million

The repercussions of those two deals are that the football rich list will be taking an increasing English feel over the coming years. However, even with the current Premier League dominance, Bayern Munich have found themselves behind only one English side – Manchester United – in the rankings of world's most valuable clubs, positioned fourth. Dortmund and Schalke both make the top fifteen of the *Forbes'* 2015 list whilst the two Spanish giants top the table. Real lead Barcelona, while Bayern are followed by Man City, Chelsea, Arsenal and Liverpool – but are some way ahead of those English rivals.

Bayern – whose value is calculated to be £1.5billion by Forbes – are some £600million ahead of City in fifth, the Blues valued at £906million. By adopting some Manchester United-style hyperactive marketing, and continuing to explore corporate functions at the Allianz Arena a la Arsenal's use of the Emirates, they can remain a major world player – with the Bundesliga's business model offering a safeguard against a fall from grace.

Chapter 5

For Dortmund, ranked 11th most valuable at £459million, and Schalke, 14th at £375million, the reality is that they are going to be overtaken by English rivals – and the gap between them and Bayern will widen. Something we will explore in more depth in *Chapter 13*.

Forbes' list of most valuable football clubs, 2015

Rank	Team	Nation	Value
1	Real Madrid	Spain	£2.14billion
2	Barcelona	Spain	£2.07billion
3	Man United	England	£2.03billion
4	Bayern Munich	Germany	£1.5billion
5	Man City	England	£906million
6	Chelsea	England	£899million
7	Arsenal	England	£860million
8	Liverpool	England	£644million
9	Juventus	Italy	£549million
10	AC Milan	Italy	£509million
11	Dortmund	Germany	£459million
12	PSG	France	£416million
13	Tottenham	England	£393million
14	Schalke	Germany	£375million
15	Inter	Italy	£288million

The level of debt on the above list, though, is telling. Third-placed Manchester United have debts of 20% of their value, while Arsenal in 7th carry 30% of their value in debt. Bayern, as you may have guessed, have zero – along with billionaire owned Man City and Chelsea, although each would owe their owners substantial sums in the case of a takeover. AC Milan in 10th have a 44% debt-to-value ratio, while city rivals Inter in 15th have 56%. By contrast, Dortmund have a debt level of 6% and Schalke are debt-free.

Those low debt levels are commonplace throughout the German league, with strict controls that prevent clubs being excessively in hock to the bank, or otherwise. And this isn't just endless handwringing or empty threats, it's a condition of earning a Football League license. When applying, clubs will be – and continue to be for renewed status – analysed by the DFL, to see if their financial status permits them to be a member club. Failure to comply with the guidelines will result in a fine, points deduction, transfer embargo or even enforced relegation.

In 1965, Hertha Berlin had their license revoked for financial irregularities and, more recently, the likes of Dynamo Dresden, Fortuna Dusseldorf, Rot-Weiss Essen, and SV Mannheim were demoted for various reasons – mainly for being unable to meet the financial forecasts published in their submitted accounts. In many ways, the Bundesliga came up with the original Financial Fair Play – UEFA's dabble with financial prudency, which Michel Platini agreed to "ease" after just four years, following criticism from the continent's elite. Punishments for Middle Eastern-backed Manchester City and Paris Saint-Germain had set a bold precedent, but UEFA was unable to stick to its guns, bowing to pressure and legal threats.

In Germany, there's no such controversy over financial monitoring – it's the done thing. Clubs live within their means, with transfers rarely financed through debt or credit. Even Bayern Munich avoid the temptation of financing transfers through bank loans – everything is funded through current assets. In the 2012/13 campaign, 17 of the 18 clubs in the Bundesliga were completely debt-free. By contrast, the same number of Premier League teams were in the red that season. Chelsea's net debt exceeded £1billion for the first time in 2015.

The 2013/14 season was the tenth in succession in which the Bundesliga recorded financial growth, with revenue rising 12.9% to €2.45billion. That meant that 13 of the 18 top-flight teams recorded a profit, one up on the previous year. While 24 of the 36 sides in the top two tiers made post-tax profit, the 2. Bundesliga reached revenue of €458million.

Even more impressively, in the context of the Premier League, was that the Bundesliga's wages/revenue ratio fell below 50% for the first time since 2006/07 in 2015 – the only 'big five' league to have done so since 1997. The season before, Premier League clubs had spent an average of 71% - while relegated QPR gambled on regaining top-flight status by spending a staggering 195% of their turnover on wages, which worked, only for them to go down again the following season. This approach to promotion to the big time is clearly common in the English Championship, as the average wages/revenue ratio was 105% in 2015.

Even the biggest of the Bundesliga's big boys is now debt free – Bayern Munich selling an 8.33% stake to Allianz which would allow the club to pay off all remaining debt on their stadium, the Allianz Arena, built in 2005, and fund investment into new youth and junior training facilities. Despite the deal – and similar agreements with Audi and Adidas – club members retain 75% of Munich's shares, as per the 50+1 rule. The football club is run by the spin-off organisation 'Bayern München AG' as a joint stock company, with the supervisory board including representatives from Adidas, Allianz and Audi.

Dortmund, too, are in rude financial health. At the end of the 2012/13 campaign, when they finished as runners up in the Champions League and Bundesliga, it wasn't just the club's shirts that shimmered gold – their coffers, too, were dazzling. They logged a net profit of €51.2million, with bottom line earnings rising by around 86% on the season before. It made for the best financial result in their entire history, and meant that investors would see their dividends raised six to ten cents per share. Only a season earlier, the club had paid out its first dividend since turning public in 2000 – the ship finally steadied for good after a financial meltdown that almost ruined the club, the full story of which will follow in *Chapter 7*.

Such success can only be good news for the second richest division in the world, just behind the Premier League, especially as television revenues are likely to climb in a similar fashion to their English counterparts, with a new deal that took the Bundesliga into the lucrative American and Asian markets from the 2015/16 season. It's a huge leap for the league, as subscription-based revenues have taken a long time to get up and running; the league's CEO Christian Seifert explains: "The TV market in Germany is very special. When pay TV was introduced in 1991, the average household already received 34 channels for free. Therefore we had the most competitive free TV market in the world.

"So this influenced the growth of pay TV very much. We were forced to show all of the 612 games of the Bundesliga and second Bundesliga live on pay TV, so we have to carry the production costs of this."

But, while the league's commercial department is busy spreading the Bundesliga gospel far and wide, there are limits to what revenue streams they are prepared to exploit. Certainly, there'll be no mooting of a foreign-hosted league game any time soon.

The Premier League's disastrous 39th game is the most notorious of such suggestions across Europe's 'big five', but the French Super Cup tie has taken place outside of the country since 2009 – when Bordeaux defeated Guingamp in Canada. Since then, the fixture has been held in Tunisia, Morocco, the United States, Gabon and China, before returning to Montreal for 2015. When announcing that the tie would be held internationally for the first time, the President of the French Football League, Frederic Thiriez, explained: "The goal is to promote French football abroad. It is time for French football to conquer new markets… Montreal, the second largest French-speaking agglomeration in the world, is an ideal gateway to North America."

Similarly, in Italy, the Supercoppa Italiana has been held overseas on several occasions – first, in Washington, in 1993, before returning to America in 2003. They headed to Beijing in 2009, 2011, and 2012, while the 2014 iteration took place in Qatar, in front of just 14,000 fans.

Germany, publicly at least, has no intention of following suit. Seifert says: "We have a completely different approach about our idea of German football. For the financial side, it would be maybe a good idea to play a match day all over the world, but not for the supporters who are visiting 34 games of that club, no matter if it's snow or rain or wind or whatever, and they're travelling. And on that game that has the impact that the team is going to be relegated and they cannot be there, because it's in Thailand, I think this would not be an approach for the Bundesliga."

So who benefits from a well-run league, which is financially responsible and realistic in its approach to transfer fees and wages? Well, everyone, but mostly the supporters – who enjoy a rare modern privilege of actually being a major consideration for Bundesliga clubs in their policies and approaches. It's little wonder that it has become the best-attended league in world football. In Germany, the fan is still king…

Chapter 6
Fan frenzy: Fan = friend, see?

Germany's Bundesliga is widely considered to be the most fan friendly division in world football, earning plaudits and set as the aspirational bar for the global game. And it's not just nice stories of beer and atmosphere.

Borussia Dortmund – the recipients of such lavish praise in *Chapter 7* – actually boasted the best average attendance in the whole of European football during the 2014/15 season, despite an underwhelming campaign where they flirted with relegation before recovering to finish 7th. More than a million BVB supporters graced the Westfalenstadion over the course of the season, averaging a crowd of more than 80,000 at each home game. That puts them ahead even of the all-conquering Barcelona, and the Catalans' huge Nou Camp venue.

A crucial reason for Dortmund's vast appeal, their famous Yellow Wall of a terrace, which has become an iconic and recognisable image throughout the game, is something that CEO Hans-Joachim Watzke has conceded actually costs the club money: "We have made some fundamental decisions to do things that we consider part of our football culture. We forgo between €4.5m and €5m every year because of terracing, but it's part of who we are."

That sacrifice, though, preserves Dortmund's identity – allowing the Südtribüne to be full of genuine, passionate fans rather than exploiting its popularity by hawking posh seats to tourists – and they reap the benefit with their table-topping crowds. And, while the standings of best-attended European stadiums were littered with the continent's giants – Barcelona, Manchester United, and Real Madrid following Dortmund on the list – there is a strong German presence.

According to *WorldFootball.net*'s calculations, four of the top ten are Bundesliga sides – with Bayern (5th, averaging 72,882), Schalke (6th, averaging 61,578), and Hamburg (8th, 53,252) all following Dortmund into the top ten. In all, seven Bundesliga teams attracted an average attendance of more than 50,000 fans, compared to just three English sides (United, Arsenal, and Newcastle), two Spanish outfits (Barca and Real), and one French club (Marseille).

As a league, the Bundesliga is streets ahead in terms of average attendance – with around 7,000 more fans per league match than the Premier League. While their crowds are almost double the size of those in the France's Ligue 1 or Italy's Serie A. All this while having seventy odd league games fewer per season – which is the only reason Germany trails in one area, the total number of fans who have attended over the course of the season. If the Bundesliga were made up of 20 teams, like the rest of the big five leagues, they'd comfortably top that table, too.

And, globally, that makes the Bundesliga the second best attended league in *any* sport – behind only the NFL, which averaged an astonishing 68,776 spectators per game in 2014. While it's probably no surprise that Bayern Munich and Borussia Dortmund often sell-out, nine other Bundesliga clubs managed to fill their capacities by more than 90 per cent over the course of the 2013/14 season. Empty seats are a real rarity in Germany.

Best-attended teams in Europe, 2014/15

Rank	Team	Total fans	Home games	Average attendance
1	Borussia Dortmund	1.367m	17	80,463
2	FC Barcelona	1.475m	19	77,632
3	Manchester United	1.431m	19	75,335
4	Real Madrid	1.388m	19	73,081
5	Bayern Munich	1.239m	17	72,882
6	FC Schalke 04	1.046m	17	61,578
7	Arsenal	1.079m	19	59,992
8	Hamburger SV	905,278	17	53,252
9	Olympique Marseille	1.005m	19	52,917
10	Newcastle United	956,823	19	50,359

Best-attended leagues in Europe, 2014/15

Rank	Team	Total fans	Matches played	Average attendance
1	Bundesliga	13.323m	306	43,539
2	Premier League	13.686m	380	36,176
3	La Liga	10.268m	380	27,021
4	Ligue Un	8.441m	380	22,215
5	Serie A	8.183m	380	22,213

*

It's difficult to deny the growing assertion that Germany has got it 'right' when it comes to fandom, with Premier League chiefs probably sick of British fans comparing their league to the Bundesliga.

Two of the most obvious differences from attending a game in Germany to one in England are that you can stand at games – with Dortmund's Südtribüne the most famous terrace, but standing areas are par for the course across the country – and that supporters are permitted to drink in the stands. At half-time, and throughout the game, beer sellers are on tap, as it were, to refill fans' drinks. Premier League games, in comparison, are often alcohol-free zones for hours in advance, the rationale being to limit the danger of violence. Yet Bundesliga games couldn't be friendlier – while their English counterparts are separated by lines of police officers, German fans of any allegiance mix freely before, during, and after the football.

But if those are the headlines, there's plenty more to the story. Also universal in the division is more accessible ticket prices. According to the *BBC's Price of Football* survey in 2014, the cheapest tickets sold by Bayern, Dortmund, Schalke and Leverkusen were all under £13. A ticket to one of the Premier League's big four, meanwhile, would be double that at cheapest – and Chelsea's lowest priced offering was the same price as Dortmund's most expensive. While the cheapest season ticket on offer at champions Bayern Munich was £103 – by comparison, the costliest offered at Arsenal was £2,013.

Not that the Premier League is home to the most exorbitant tickets in Europe – AC Milan's most expensive season ticket was priced at £3,600, and Paris St-Germain's equivalent was £2,115. And match day tickets are also pricey at Milan, with AC's highest price point £298 – Arsenal's is 'just' £97.

La Liga giants Barcelona and Real Madrid impress with their cheapest match day tickets, both around £18, but their priciest are more than three times the cost of the equivalents at Dortmund or Munich – BVB's costing around £50, while Real's is £184. And Barcelona's cheapest season ticket, at £105, just about bests Bayern's equivalent, but is only open to club members. Becoming a 'socio' requires a stringent process; in Germany, becoming a supporter couldn't be easier, or, much cheaper.

Overall, Bundesliga prices are favourable when compared to most in Europe – particularly against other leagues in the big five. The Dortmund versus Arsenal comparison is a regular one but – sorry Gunners fans – it is actually a parallel with Bayern that illustrates the gulf most succinctly: the cost of one of Arsenal's cheapest season tickets (£1,014) would be enough to purchase almost *ten* of Bayern's equivalent.

Even better, ticket prices can also cover supporters' transport costs in Germany – with match day tickets eligible for free use of public transport for several hours before and after the game – a service that is facilitated and subsidised by the clubs.

Explaining why German teams keep prices low – even though they could get away with ramping them up – Christian Seifert, CEO of the DFL, said: "We value the fan culture we have. We are the last of the big leagues with standing areas and nobody wants to touch these standing areas. The clubs are committed to having many cheap tickets, because it is considered very important in Germany that people who do not have very much money are able to come to the stadium.

"Here, football is one of the last activities which really brings people together, across all ages and all classes of income. Politics does not do it, the church does not make it happen. Most chairmen and chief executives have been very much involved with football, they have been supporters and players. They see from a pure business perspective they could raise prices and make more money. But they have decided to take less money and enable people whose families have supported the club for generations, and young people, to keep coming. We want to have our whole society as part of our football, in our stadiums."

It's an approach that has pushed many British fans towards German football – see *Chapter 8* for some examples – and Dortmund have noticed the influx of British fans to their games. Marketing director Carsten Cramer said: "It's amazing. It's always nice when English fans tell me that including the cost of a flight, two beers and a ticket, they do not pay more than a match in England." The club have even had to start conducting their stadium tours in English to cater for the demand of their new fan base.

Ticket prices for 2014/15

Team	League	Cheapest match day ticket	Most expensive	Cheapest season ticket	Most expensive
Bayern Munich	Bundesliga	£11.75	£54.82	£109.65	£587.38
Dortmund	Bundesliga	£12.84	£50.09	£159.77	£552.53
Schalke	Bundesliga	£12.14	£48.56	£149.20	£607.75
Leverkusen	Bundesliga	£11.75	£53.26	£133.14	£422.92
Arsenal	Premier League	£27	£97	£1,014	£2,013
Man City	Premier League	£37	£58	£299	£860
Chelsea	Premier League	£50	£87	£750	£1,250
Man United	Premier League	£36	£58	£532	£950
Barcelona	La Liga	£18.01	£153.50	£103.38	£859.15
Real Madrid	La Liga	£18.80	£184.05	£174.65	£1,441.05
Atletico	La Liga	£15.66	£140.97	£254.53	£857.58
Athletic	La Liga	£19.58	£86.15	£234.95	£1,069.82
Valencia	La Liga	£7.83	£46.99	£156.64	£1,076.87
AC Milan	Serie A	£16.34	£298.05	£162.69	£3,597.92

Team	League	Cheapest match day ticket	Most expensive	Cheapest season ticket	Most expensive
Inter	Serie A	£19.56	£195.53	£156.43	£1,720.74
Juventus	Serie A	£19.56	£109.50	£305.03	£1,094.98
PSG	Ligue 1	£11.75	£172.30	£336.77	£2,114.59
PSV	Dutch Eredivisie	£19.54	£54.71	£197.39	£422.08
Anderlecht	Belgian Pro League	£25	£36.72	£140.68	£343.83

Talking about the gulf in pricing priorities, Bayern's former chairman Uli Hoenness famously surmised it as: "We could charge more than £104 [for a season ticket] – let's say we charged £300, we'd get £2million more in income. But what's £2million to us? In a transfer discussion, you argue about that sum for five minutes, but the difference between £104 and £300 is huge for the fan.

"We do not think fans are like cows who you milk, football has got to be for everybody. That's the biggest difference between us and England."

This was on the back of his side meeting Arsenal in the Champions League in 2014, having subsidised the cost of tickets for their fans, after being shocked at the price set by their hosts. With the Gunners charging visiting fans €75 a head to watch the game, on top of travel and accommodation, which is far from cheap in London, Bayern intervened to contribute around €90,000 towards ticket costs – reducing each ticket to €45. It wasn't a move to ensure fans turned up – the club received more than 18,000 applications for just 2,974 tickets. Bayern did not have to intervene.

In a statement posted on the club website, they explained their decision: "The terrific support of the fans lifted Bayern [during the previous season, when they won a treble]. Particularly noteworthy is the large number of Bayern fans who not only supported the highlights but were at every game.

"The fact is that this loyalty at such a high number of games does not only take up a great deal of time, but it also tears a big hole in the wallet. This [subsidy] is intended as a small thank you for your great support in 2013."

The return leg saw Bayern's prices range between £12 and £50 – markedly cheaper than Arsenal's £62 price-point for away supporters – and drew plaudits from fans of both teams involved in the tie. Nordi Chaoui-Taylor, spokesman for Arsenal fans' group Black Scarf Movement, said at the time: "We commend Bayern's gesture and, once again, this demonstrates that, in Germany, the core support of clubs is truly recognised and taken care of.

"In this country [England], it seems as if clubs are more focused on greed, looking to take their own fans for as much as they possibly can. We believe this short-term dash for cash is ultimately damaging for English football in the longer term. It's time those running our clubs take the blinkers off and look at the bigger picture."

Dortmund, too, have had several eye-opening visits to North London in European competition. And the facilities they would've experienced in 2012/3 and 2014/5 – while impressive and state of the art – would have been used in a totally different way to their own.

The Emirates was designed specifically to maximise corporate facilities and opportunities, with the different customer tiers receiving varying degrees of comfort. In the plush hospitality boxes, for instance, where a three course buffet meal is served with a mini bar stocked high with booze, punters can remain indoors when the action kicks off on the pitch – the only proviso is that the box's blinds are lowered while they continue drinking.

For those involved in the running of Dortmund, this is the antithesis to what they're trying to do. A case in point: like the Emirates, the Westfalenstadion has its own stadium WiFi – though access is free in Dortmund – but the signal is dipped once the match begins to ensure the fans' focus is on the game. Likewise, Dortmund do not sell drinks in their corporate boxes during the game – preserving throats for singing rather than boozing. Not that they need worry about volume levels while the Südtribüne is sold out.

The huge terrace rises up at a steep incline, and is filled by 25,000 supporters. To take your place amongst them, you'll inevitably have to squeeze past several hundred people to climb to a suitable spot. Contradicting the stereotype of German efficiency, there's no set spots here to stand – you're thrown amongst a crowd, and left to work it out between yourselves.

In England, you could imagine this sort of set up being monitored and policed by an army of stewards. Instead, the German fans just get on with it. There's no agro, no fuss – there'll be room enough for everyone. Once you've found a suitable spot to claim, you form part of a live, moving organism. As the person in front of you shuffles to their left, you follow suit, letting another fan past. This is constant, especially for those lining the stairs.

Once the game has kicked off, the entire terrace seems to bounce as one – egged on by official 'cheerleaders' perched high up on platforms above the goal. The sound seems to reverberate inside you, even from outside the stadium, and you can't help but get swept along with it. When Dortmund score, you're likely to be drenched in beer, as hundreds of excitable fans toss their plastic cups into the air in glee. Visiting the famous south stand is an experience that has to be seen – and heard – to be believed.

And it's something that other Bundesliga clubs are eagerly trying to recreate. Bayern Munich's Allianz Arena has Stehplätze – standing room – behind either goalmouth, with blocks 112 and 113 converted to terracing before the 2006/07 season after complaints from the club's ultras. These sections are reseated for UEFA or international matches, where regulations demand that games are all-seater, but the terracing is restored for domestic fixtures.

On average, there are 10,000 standing fans at every Bundesliga game, with half of the division's clubs using 'rail seats', which lock upright leaving rows of standing areas with built-in safety barriers – and can easily be converted back to seating for UEFA fixtures. This innovation – first used by Werder Bremen in the early 2000s – is being hailed as the future of safe standing areas.

The popularity of this futuristic terracing in Germany has been a factor in the growing campaign for the reintroduction of standing areas at top-flight football matches in England – with all-seaters introduced in the aftermath of the Hillsborough disaster. The Liberal Democrats pledged to bring back terraces for Premier League and Championship stadiums in the 2015 General Election campaign, claiming that 92% of English fans and the majority of Football

League clubs – who said it would generate a better atmosphere – backed the idea. If they needed an example of why famous terraces such as Aston Villa's old Holte End should return to England, they need only look at the Bundesliga.

For many German football fans, preserving these terracing sections is a way of protecting their national game's identity. Such a decision reflects the fan power prevalent in the country – the dominant force, Bayern Munich, backing down over protests from a small section of their support.

In November 2012, Dortmund's usually raucous fan base were eerily silent for the first twelve minutes and twelve seconds of a Bundesliga clash with Fortuna Düsseldorf in protest at new security proposals which were perceived to challenge the future of standing areas. Politicians in Germany often threaten an all-seater culture akin to that of England – something that has majorly underwhelmed German fans.

Nicolai Maurer, part of Dortmund's Unity ultras group, explained the objections to *The Guardian*, saying: "If there are some problems at the stadium, we do not believe the answer is repression. The politicians are threatening that Germany must have seats and we are worried it will be like England, where the football atmosphere was famous, but now it is so quiet.

"At Manchester City it was a little better, but at Arsenal last year we could not believe you could football so quietly. We don't want that."

Perhaps most surprising about that Dortmund protest is that the club itself helped facilitate it – supplying staff to let ultras into the stadium four hours before kick-off so they could lay leaflets explaining their campaign on the seats. The Bundesliga, against whom the protest was aimed, also enabled the fans their say; the Fan-Projekt team of social workers (which the Bundesliga help to fund) delivered the leaflets, banners and flags to the stadium.

Explaining the surprisingly diplomatic culture, Dortmund supporter liaison officer Jens Volke, described as a former "chief of our ultra fans" by Hans-Joachim Watzke, said: "This is [the fans'] opinion, so we believe we should support free speech. It is a policy of the club. We want young people to come here, to feel included, and we work with them to help them use their energy in a positive way. They are not outsiders, they are part of the club."

Even chief executive Watzke backed the fan protest. A lifelong Dortmund supporter, he said at the time: "This is our German football culture – to have standing and cheap tickets and the clubs controlled by their members. We want everybody to feel it is their club and that is really important.

"I was a supporter standing for 20 years, I know what it is to stand there, the feeling, the discussions you have there. In Germany, we are a little bit romantic. Where there is a club, the German supporter wants to have the feeling it is his club – not the club of Qatar or Abu Dhabi."

Such issues are raised by supporter liaison officers like Volke, who are employed by clubs to work specifically on fan issues and interests – representing the fans in board meetings, and providing the voice of the faithful when big decisions are made. It's even been known for potential signings to be run past these individuals, to gauge fan reaction to a potentially controversial acquisition.

This link between club and support is a valuable one for all involved – and one that fans of English teams surely envy. Imagine if the early days of Mike Ashley's controversial regime at Newcastle had included a fan representative. Various PR own goals could have been avoided, and supporters would have felt informed – rather than ignored and left out in the cold.

Likewise, Cardiff City's controversial decision to change home colours from blue to red – though it has now been reversed – might have been avoided if owner Vincent Tan had heard the fans' side of the story earlier. And the desperation of Hull City owner Assem Allam to rename the club as the 'Hull Tigers', *might* have been lessened had he employed a supporter liaison officer – though it seems unlikely. But even clubs with less contentious issues to deal with could improve their bond with supporters.

Meinolf Sprink, Director of Communications and Media at Bayer Leverkusen, explained the role of SLOs at his club during an interview for this book. He said: "We are a club playing at the Champions League level, and we employ four full time supporter liaison officers. We also have a project called The Fan Project, which is focussed on social work, financed by the league and the city of Leverkusen, as well as the club.

"The main role of an SLO is to be the contact person to our supporter clubs and supporters in general, to focus on *all* supporters who might have questions or problems. Also, on match-day, the SLOs of both clubs will talk to the police 45 minutes before a game starts to prepare for something that might happen, but will not happen because of this briefing.

"On top of that, there is also a group of 150 volunteers who are involved in the handling of a game day – with the focus of being visible to our supporters and of the opponent club.

"The role of the SLO is all about communication. I meet with them twice a week, and we sit down together for two hours and talk about everything – what the fans need from the club, what challenges they face, problems they've had, issues with transport.

"It's an ongoing process, to ensure the supporters have, at some point, the ear of the club. It's clear to all of our supporters that these four people – the SLOs – are people they can trust, and who will help them as much as possible: whether that's with match security, travelling to an away match, etc.

"When it comes to decision making, it's a golden rule that we include the four representatives and inform them in advance of what might happen, and provide them with a clear message if we have something. The fan and supporter clubs will receive such news before the media: We are signing a new player, someone might be fired, the ticket prices might change.

"During the process, they are involved – if we are considering raising the prices, we are eager to have a first and very honest reaction and opinions from the SLOs, because they have a better feeling if it is something that the supporters can deal with, or if they have objections.

"For instance, we have just raised prices for the first time in seven years, by about ten per cent, but the fans have applauded this decision, because they understand why – we have improved the facilities and experience.

"Having SLOs is a no-brainer, and we've been doing it for many years – if you don't keep close contact with your supporters, you lose them. As a works club, our fans are maybe more democratic, and more rational than emotional.

"We are communicating in a clear way, so the fans feel comfortable with the running of the club. In the last couple of years, we have rarely had any problems."

After a UEFA ruling, inspired by the Bundesliga model, in 2010, English teams have had to follow suit – after it was made mandatory for clubs to employ an SLO. A handful of Football League sides even have two, though Dortmund's team of SLOs is a five-man operation – and English clubs have yet to let these fan reps into boardroom discussions. But it is a step in the right direction.

Other English envies might revolve around match day highlights. Though we have national institution *Match of the Day*, and are quite content with that, German football fans go one better. While our round-up show is late night, they see every goal on public television an hour after Saturday's matches have ended. In the UK, that right is reserved for those paying a subscription fee. Likewise, the first game of the Bundesliga season – the champions starting the defence of their crown – and the first game after the winter break, are both shown live on free TV. No Premier League game is shown live on terrestrial television.

And the players are equally accessible in Germany. Almost every training session at Bayern Munich is open to supporters to watch. The only exception to this is the final session before a match when the manager, understandably, wants to reveal his specific game plan in private. It is something that seems impossible in Britain – just try approaching a club's training ground and see how far you get. Arsenal's London Colney facility is like a fortress.

Similarly, there's little such division between opposing sets of fans. In the build up to the 2013 Champions League final, Bayern and Dortmund met in a domestic encounter just weeks before the showpiece event at Wembley. With the visitors from Munich having already wrapped up the league title a month earlier, and antagonised their hosts by announcing the imminent capture of star player Mario Götze – a deal that left the club "disappointed beyond measure", according to chief executive Hans-Joachim Watzke – there was plenty of edge to the clash.

Indeed, on field, the teams played out a niggly 1-1 draw, with Brazilian midfielder Rafinha's sending off prompting a touchline bust-up with Jürgen Klopp, but the sell-out crowd arrived and left the stadium together – with many arm in arm with their so-called rivals, even sharing chants of *"Football's coming home"* together, referring to their European rematch in England. Coming from the Premier League, where away fans are regularly locked away in their sections for hours after the match, it is a staggering sight to walk to such a high-profile game amid a genuinely mixed crowd in Germany.

Fans drink and talk together before and after the match regardless of allegiance. The passion is clear, but there's little air of the tribalism that often blights equivalent English fixtures. All in, match days are a far more enjoyable and affordable experience in the Bundesliga than they are in the Premier League.

*

If Germany are leading the way, the Bundesliga's trailblazer is Dortmund – the club earning cult status and drawing support from around the world for its mentality and philosophy, rather than glamour and big name signings. It is there that much of Germany's recent success is best exemplified and produced...

Chapter 7
Bor-illiant Dortmund

The club that has come to symbolise all that is right with German football, with its home-grown emphasis, responsible ticket pricing, and the buoyant atmosphere of the 'Yellow Wall' – the huge, and now very famous, South Bank where up to 25,000 fans stand and roar their beloved team on – is Borussia Dortmund. In terms of footballing world wonders, a Dortmund match is very much on the list of must-see treasures.

And the club has plenty to sing about. Having undergone a fall from grace that serves as a warning against the English-style excesses of throwing money at football, the side with the iconic yellow kit have returned to the fore with a similar rebuilding process to the national game in general. After a golden period during the late Nineties, when the club reached its first Champions League final, where 20-year-old local boy Lars Ricken scored the winner – proof that some philosophies have long been rooted in Germany – and lifting the Bundesliga title three times, Dortmund made the controversial move to become the country's first – and only – publicly traded club on the stock market.

As a business decision, it actually worked out well, initially, earning the club a windfall. However, the pressure of being crowned European champions told, and the newfound wealth burned a hole in their pocket. Suddenly, Dortmund felt compelled to act as the biggest clubs in the world do – namely, spend a lot of money, and recklessly. But such poorly managed expenditure came back to bite BVB hard, with their soaring debt levels compounded by a failure to qualify for the 2004 Champions League – having also been knocked out in the qualifying round the previous year.

That meant missing out on a cut of the competition's lucrative television money twice; so often it is the financial gravy train that can make or break a club that has staked everything on its entry, just look at Leeds United in England.

Indicative of the Dortmund approach at the time was splurging a national record €25million on Parma's striker Márcio Amoroso in the summer of 2001. At first, it appeared to be a worthwhile investment, with the Brazilian finishing top scorer as Dortmund lifted the Bundesliga title, in addition to reaching the UEFA Cup final in his first season at the club. They were still a major player in Europe, and the main force in Germany, and their lavish new signing had produced the goods.

But Amoroso's prolific record tailed off after that debut term, and he mustered just ten league goals over the next two seasons. Indeed, the club ended up cancelling his contract after a series of bust-ups and injuries, as they were desperate to get him off the wage bill as panic set in around the absence of Champions League funds. This was done with good reason; they were about to embark on a nine-year absence from the competition.

Manager Matthias Sammer paid the price, and was also shown the door, as his side could only reach sixth in the table, missing out on European football entirely. His successor, Dutchman Bert van Marwijk from Feyenoord, was the first of three managers employed in as many years, as BVB plummeted.

On the field, Amoroso wasn't the only star to prove troublesome at a time when everything seemed to be going wrong for Dortmund – Jens Lehmann had been sold to Arsenal the season before, after a mixed time at the club, part of an unruly dressing room that lacked discipline. And, a month before Amoroso's contract was terminated, Nigerian international Sunday Oliseh was sacked after either punching or head-butting a teammate while on loan at Bochum. Also moved on in the summer of 2004 was Germany midfielder Torsten Frings, poached by Bayern Munich for €10million, whom he promptly helped to a domestic double. As the black hole in Dortmund's bank balance grew larger, the first team was stripped of saleable assets.

It wasn't just members of the playing staff that were sold off to cut costs. The club's stadium and most valuable saleable asset, the Westfalenstadion, was sold to a real estate trust to generate funding, while players were forced to take a mandatory 20% pay cut. Incredibly, Bayern even stepped in to loan their rivals €2million to ensure that wages were paid for a couple of months.

With the financial crisis of 2005, Dortmund found themselves on the brink of insolvency – their shares having plummeted 80% in value – only for a last minute restructuring package to dramatically save the club. This collapse had meant that Dortmund were unable to continue paying agreed instalments to rebuy their stadium. Thankfully, the holders of the trust reduced interest rates and agreed to delayed payments once the club's restructuring had taken place, which not only saved Dortmund from bankruptcy, but also automatic demotion to amateur football, and a long, hard road back to the top.

The group that held this decisive power wasn't some huge conglomerate, but an assembly of small-time investors that had put money into the club through an investment fund. They could have demanded their money back immediately, cutting their losses on a now unlikely looking profit, and put the club out of business. Instead, they unwittingly prompted the creation of one of world football's most popular outfits.

Their generosity also meant that the stadium would be reunited with its rightful owners. Dortmund bought the Westfalenstadion back in 2006, with a loan from American bank Morgan Stanley. To manage this debt, the club agreed sponsorship with a local insurance company, renaming the stadium Signal Iduna Park until 2021.

As it re-emerged, burned but not obliterated by the flames of its mismanagement, Dortmund did so with renewed philosophies, which matched those set out at a national level. Primarily, they sought to invest in youth and develop their own talent – doing so would improve the club's performance on and off the pitch, as talents could be moved on in money-spinning deals. A case in point was the discovery of Shinji Kagawa in Japan, who cost Dortmund €350,000 in 2010 – two years later, they sold him to Manchester United for a reported £17million.

In fact, barely a year after coming close to oblivion, Dortmund were showing a profit again – fuelled by the sale of Tomas Rosicky to Arsenal, amongst others. It was a symbolic transfer in many ways. When the Czech schemer had arrived at Dortmund in 2001, he had been the Bundesliga's most expensive ever signing, at £18million, and was indicative of the club's approach. His departure, then, heralded a shift in focus on transfer policy towards the home-grown

Chapter 7

– a change overseen by incoming chairman Hans-Joachim Watzke, introduced by the parent company, effectively, to save Dortmund.

What he found upon his arrival at the ailing club was not to his liking, with the philosophy geared around off-field matters rather than success on the pitch. Speaking recently, he said: "In a prospectus which was published for the shareholders in 2000 or 2001, I saw that Borussia Dortmund were 'seeking to develop other business activities in order to become independent from sporting success'. It was the greatest rubbish I've read in my entire life. If you stink on the pitch, it'll never work. Which is why our credo now is: it's only about football.

"There's a headline above everything that we do. That headline is: we want to have maximum sporting success, but we will never again go into debt for it. In only 18 months, we cut our budget from €57million to €24million. The problem was that people still thought of us as a Champions League club and that 75,000 or so came to watch the home games. But we didn't have the team anymore to meet these expectations. The older players were mentally already on the hop, looking for new clubs."

As well as off-field restructuring, Watzke wanted to re-examine the club's entire philosophy, which was virtually non-existent – like many of Europe's leading lights, it was simply to spend big in the transfer market, and hope that ensured success. But they were never going to out-Bayern Bayern, not over a prolonged period, anyway. Instead, they needed to define what it was to be 'Dortmund'.

"We sat down and first had a look at the status quo. Then we asked ourselves: what is it people expect in this part of the country, the working-class Ruhr area? The answer was that they expect an honest effort and that you give your all. So that informed our new philosophy. We defined the brand as: real and intense. The football should be intense, while we should be real."

Part of this plan was to rely on younger, local players. Though this was guided as much by necessity as it was by ideology; with costs to cut, Dortmund had little choice but to ship out the players on big wages, and hope that cheaper alternatives would work. It was a prompt about-turn; as the club had previously channelled most of their funding into transfer fees and wages rather than a youth system.

When the DFB threatened Dortmund with relegation if they didn't shape up imminently – namely, build an actual training complex – the club was left with no choice but to commit to a similar sort of plan to the one dictating policy at a national level. Luckily for them, it just so happened that local talent was emerging at exactly that point, and the decision became easier to embrace when the scale of the potential at their disposal became apparent. In August 2005, Nuri Sahin became the club and league's youngest ever player – and, three months later, the youngest goalscorer in Bundesliga history – at the age of 16, having joined Dortmund as a 13-year-old boy.

Suddenly, a philosophy had been born, and priorities had been reversed. Now, the club wanted to play the patient game, and nurture talent like Sahin through a proper youth system – led by the hero of 1997, Lars Ricken, who is now a Youth Coordinator at the club.

Meeting him for this book, behind the scenes at Dortmund's training ground, he explains enthusiastically: "Our philosophy is not to sign a lot of international players, but concentrate on those from within an 80 kilometre radius of Dortmund. It's important for young players to have their social network around them as they develop – over the last twenty years, it's this sort of player we've seen do best.

"I was born in Dortmund, Mario Götze grew up here from the age of six. That's also important for the identification between fans and players. It's a deep relationship, hence the atmosphere at our games."

Fellow Youth Coordinator Edwin 'Eddy' Boekamp – a popular character at the club, whose involvement dates back decades across various positions – revealed the extent of the success achieved by the club's youth system: "Many of our young players make it. Not only at Dortmund but throughout the first and second division – currently there are more than 40 players from our academy. We have one of the highest conversions in the country."

Dortmund's nondescript training facility, Hohenbuschei, wouldn't immediately strike a visitor as the main production line of German football's superstars. In fact, when pulling up to the training ground, it feels like you could be parking in front of any old office block. There's certainly no high-security entrance like you'd find at certain Premier League outfits.

At the centre of the state-of-the-art complex is a building that houses changing rooms, offices, a gym and a canteen, surrounded by eight training pitches, which vary in terms of surface and size. To the right of the beige hub are full media and press conference facilities, while to the left is a similar-looking building which homes up to 22 youth players who live on site. These boys are youngsters who have been scouted from further away, for whom a commute to and from training would be arduous. Local lads are either placed with local families or continue to live at home - as Mario Götze did until he left the club, even as he emerged as one of the brightest talents in the country, and a first team star. Even at the age of 19, as the most hyped young talent in the Bundesliga, Götze was still having his cooking and washing done by his mother – as he remained at the family home, in a kind of studio flat set-up on the top floor of their detached house, including his own bathroom and balcony.

Similarly low key, the surroundings at Hohenbuschei might not be breathtaking, but the success stemming from the facility certainly is – Dortmund provided five members of the original 2014 World Cup winning squad – Kevin Großkreutz, Mats Hummels, Erik Durm, Roman Weidenfaller, and Marco Reus, who eventually missed the tournament through injury – plus youth graduate Götze, who left for Bayern at the start of the 2013/14 season.

But there's plenty more where he came from, Ricken insists – after a radical shake up on the back of international failures: "Euro 2000 was a total disaster, the lowest point of German football. Before that, we didn't need to have an eye on youth because our team was so strong. Since then, we've invested more than €700million into youth academies, soon it'll reach €1billion. Now, we're simply harvesting that investment."

Which is an ominous statement of intent for nations hoping to challenge Germany any time soon.

Despite the incredible achievements of Dortmund's youth system, propelling Germany to their first tournament win in 18 years, I half expect my visit to consist of boastful youngsters rubbing my nose in England's comparative failures. I know it would be if the roles were, miraculously, reversed. But that's just not the German style – there's no room for smugness, especially not at Dortmund, where even the biggest achievements are played down, and focus immediately returns to 'what's next?'.

This is brought to life perfectly by youth coach Hannes Wolf, whose Under-17 side had won their youth division in the season building up to the World Cup, proving that the future generations are scarily promising, too. Not that any of them are being allowed to get ahead of themselves.

Wolf said: "The most important thing is today - not what you did yesterday, or might do tomorrow. We have some fantastic young players here, who could go on to have great careers, but we want to concentrate on football, not all that comes with it.

"Nothing can be taken for granted in football. Just because you are champion one year, it does not mean you will be first again the next. We must not be distracted by the past."

He also tells me that players are prevented from giving media interviews – he won't identify any of his squad to me, even conversationally – because the club wants them to stay grounded and focused.

In Germany, young stars must continue attending school until they are 18, no matter how good they are – it is mandatory across the country. Those based in the 'youth house' attend a local school just around the corner from the training ground, and are monitored closely with strict curfews and dietary guidelines to stick to.

As well as a full-time school schedule, prospects juggle a full-on training programme of six sessions a week, with just Tuesdays off. That might sound like an intense timetable for young boys to manage, but the incentive for these prodigies is right on their doorstep – at Dortmund, players of all ages train, change and eat alongside one another. Status is acknowledged through respect, but it is a two-way thing, and there are no feelings of superiority towards the youngsters from senior players. These kids are the future, after all.

The club's playing and non-playing staff are described as a 'family' throughout my visit to the training ground – and the ritual is that they greet every person they meet, regardless of whether they're a first team pro, a physio, or a visiting sportswriter.

Chapter 7

I experience this protocol first hand, after arriving early for my scheduled appointment, and lingering near a training pitch where a youth team had just finished a session. As they passed me, each and every player greeted me with a polite "hallo", and clasped my hand warmly, taking a full five minutes.

Dortmund demands only the best from its players, which is a fair request given that these starlets are provided with premium facilities to hone their abilities – which cost the club around €4million a year, a serious outlay and commitment to the future. And that investment has already provided a quantifiable return, with a €1.5million secret weapon crucial in Germany's recent success.

This secret weapon is a facility, known as the 'footbonaut' – one of only two in the world, the other of which is, of course, also in Germany – which scientifically analyses players as balls are fired at them from four different directions, at eight different heights, at varying speeds from within a training cage. A sound effect indicates where the ball is coming from, before a wall panel lights up for them to shoot through. Realistic match day sound effects make it harder to hear audio cues, seeking to replicate as closely as possible the true game experience.

Watching on, as a player goes through his drills, will be a coach, offering immediate feedback on a smartphone or tablet, where they can store such information for future comparison and reference. And it was here that Germany's World Cup success was sealed – Mario Götze's athletic volley a carbon copy of what he refined in the footbonaut.

Boekamp smiled: "Mario Götze was the best at this - you could say that his goal in the World Cup final was made here. It was exactly the same. A ball coming in high, from an angle, and having to put it in a very precise position. He's been training his whole life for that moment."

And Boekamp spends his days searching – often throughout Europe – for the next Götze to emerge, with a very specific checklist of required attributes: "Yes, there are physical things we look for, skills we require, a level of fitness – but, also, their character must suit us, otherwise he has no perspective of BVB.

"There are players who come to us, asking for the world – or their advisor asking for them – and we just say no. Making teenagers millionaires is not our main policy or philosophy. They might get that if they work hard, and do what we say, but that is for tomorrow, not today."

That this admirable philosophy has emerged so rapidly, again within a 10-year timeframe, is testament to the climate in German football – but it was also fuelled by necessity. In 2000, while the national team were enduring their disaster tournament, Dortmund had no proper training facilities and the first team used a field close to the stadium, Rabenloh, as a makeshift alternative.

In one archived post on Dortmund's official website, the club appealed for information about a stolen goal frame from the dilapidated site, writing: "It is 1.80m wide and 1.40m high…relevant information please contact groundsman Willi Droste".

Despite the amateur-ish set up, Dortmund were league champions in 2002 – but short-termism still ruled, with no suitable pitch for the youth team. It wasn't until 2006, with Germany's hosting of the World Cup dominating the national discourse, that Dortmund's swish facility opened. Just three years later, Mario Götze emerged into the first team – twelve months after mainstay left back Marcel Schmelzer had made the same leap. Now, the Dortmund production line of brilliant young talents is considered a rite of passage.

*

A huge part of Dortmund's philosophy was fostered by the iconic Jürgen Klopp, who was appointed in July 2008, after a dreadful season that saw the club finish 13th. With his cool older brother vibe, the inspiring figure immediately instilled a do-or-die sense about the club on and off the field, a passion that had been lacking. His priorities for the struggling side he inherited were short-term, game-by-game, with every goal special. To this end, he shunned video footage of great teams to learn from, instead showing his dressing room photographs of the way those outfits celebrated each goal like it was their first. That was all he asked for from his team, a simple, child-like enjoyment of playing football.

85

Chapter 7

The players were unsurprisingly enthused and, within three years, they were crowned champions. The following season, they regained their crown, amassing a points tally of 81 – the biggest in Bundesliga history – as Klopp's high energy, all-action style of play took the Bundesliga by storm. Key to this was his use of 'gegenpressing', or counter pressing, which came to be their trademark. The tactic dictates that, if Dortmund lose possession near the opposition's penalty box, the group defies convention – drop off, cede territory, and start again – by pushing forward and applying immediate pressure to retrieve the ball.

It's an all or nothing approach that endeared Klopp to his fans, and Dortmund to world football – no matter what the score, it means his side set out as though they were chasing a late equalizer. His swarming forwards, though technically defending, create plenty of goals by winning the ball back in dangerous positions. When this happens, there's no tiki-taka, but a direct attack – the ball played forward immediately, capitalising on the space created by their transitioning opponents.

The cavalier tactic had to be fine-tuned slightly for European football, with ball retention important especially on off-days for your frontmen, but those tweaks clearly came easily for Klopp's men – as they reached the Champions League final in 2013, a remarkable turnaround for a side that almost went out of business barely seven years earlier. The reception 'Kloppo' received at the end of the 2014/15 season, which was actually an underwhelming campaign for the club, was testament to all of his hard work, as he bade Dortmund farewell – to be succeeded by Thomas Tuchel, as he had done at Mainz. What the incoming manager will have found is a team in need of work, but in a far healthier position than the one Klopp inherited seven years earlier.

So, now that the club has re-emerged as one of Europe's superpowers, what are Dortmund's aims and ambitions for the future? Can they remain at the pinnacle of the game, challenging in the latter stages of the Champions League, or is that reserved only for sides run by oligarchs and Arab royalty?

Financially, they've clearly recovered handsomely, having broken their club transfer record in 2013 to sign Armenian schemer Henrikh Mkhitaryan from Shakhtar, spending £20million on the playmaker.

That was a significant moment, exceeding the fee invested in Amoroso in 2001, flagging that the club had gone full circle – but were now actually in a position to part with such amounts without jeopardising their stability.

Add to that the signings of Gabon forward Pierre-Emerick Aubameyang (£11.5million) and highly regarded Greek defender Sokratis Papastathopoulos (£7million) in the same summer window, all three players purchased following the Champions League final, and it's clear the club are in a position to compete in the transfer market once more.

That spending spree didn't necessarily indicate a regression to old habits – the signings were mostly funded by the £31.5million departure of Mario Götze to Bayern, who also spent £21.5million on Thiago Alcantara. Dortmund were simply doing their best to go toe-to-toe with their rivals, having fallen just short against them at Wembley, and often losing their leading lights to them – Götze in 2013, Lewandowski in 2014.

They spent big again to replace the painful departure of Lewandowski, snapping up Italy striker Ciro Immobile for £15.5million, Adrian Ramos from Hertha Berlin (€9million), and sealing Shinji Kagawa's cut-price return from Manchester United, parting with £6million, half what they had received for him from the Red Devils two seasons earlier. Bayern might keep poaching their best players, but Dortmund are determined to keep pace with them.

Something they make no bones about, with CEO Watzke openly admitting: "Our stated aim is that the German game will not have one but two lighthouses by the year 2020, and that the second will not be red and white [Bayern's colours], as lighthouses usually are, but black and yellow [Dortmund's colours]."

Certainly, in world football, German football is the lighthouse shining brightest right now. That Champions League final meeting between Bayern and Dortmund was the moment the nation was universally acknowledged as a resurgent force. Truly, the Bundesliga had become a global phenomenon – and it's showing no signs of slowing down...

Chapter 8
Becoming a global phenomenon

If you were to believe the Premier League's marketing experts, and hype-generators in chief, there's only one league that has become a truly global division – England's top flight.

And, certainly, the biggest sides in the country possess a worldwide fan base. A Manchester United survey in 2012 claimed that the club had 659 million supporters, of which 325 million were said to be based in Asia, with a further 173 million supposedly from Africa and the Middle East. Those extraordinary – and, for some, slightly exaggerated – numbers mean that the Red Devils have more fans outside their home continent, let alone nation or city.

That purported popularity isn't confined to Old Trafford, either – with most of the Premier League eager to similarly explore foreign fan bases. Whilst the division doesn't have twenty clubs of United's size, they were still keen to host a round of matches abroad, confident that even less-glamorous ties such as Stoke versus Sunderland would still appeal to a foreign market. An idea inspired, as ever, by the NFL – who host several games a year in London, to tap into their own burgeoning overseas fan base.

Though the ill-fated '39th game' was blocked – for the time being, anyway – it showed just how vast the perceived interest in the Premier League is, something clubs are busily trying to make the most of, in efforts to open up lucrative new revenue streams.

This is, again, exemplified at Manchester United. Their American owners, the Glazer family, use the outfit purely as a business investment, and one of their key tactics has been to expand the club's marketing department enormously. Upon their arrival in Manchester, United had just two staff working on commercial tie-ups around the globe. Ten years on, they employ a department of more than 150, brokering deals with their 'soft drinks partner' in China, the

'Integrated Telecommunications Partner of Manchester United for Saudi Arabia', and even an official paint partner.

Their headline achievement was negotiating a world record £750million deal with Adidas for the sportswear giant to provide the United kit for 10 years. In the context of Financial Fair Play restrictions, the agreement – which more than trebled United's previous £23.5million-a-season deal with Nike – effectively writes off £75million of new signings each summer. And that's before the money from their Irish potato chip partner, and the like, is considered.

But, as United and the rest of the Premier League milk their global appeal for all its worth, there's an increasingly prevalent sense that they are neglecting supporters closer to home. So, while English sides have been out recruiting new fans overseas, a portion of their existing fan base has become attracted, and rather attached, to the Bundesliga. Some have even become fully-fledged supporters, with the financial implications of following a Premier League club meaning that it's more affordable to follow, say, Dortmund than Arsenal; a recent marketing email from Stansted Airport promoted a Ryanair flight to Dortmund, costing just £17.99. A train from Stansted to Highbury & Islington train station, near Arsenal's Emirates Stadium, costs from £19.60.

It's a comparison that Matthew Gerrard, 40, from Kent, himself made, with the German outfit emerging favourably. He said: "Me and a group of friends went over to Germany for the 2006 World Cup, as it isn't difficult to get to the Channel Tunnel from Kent, and then only four hours drive to the stadium.

"We went to the Brazil versus Japan game at Dortmund, and that was our first taste of German football. We were so impressed by how friendly and welcoming the people were, it changed our perceptions of German people completely.

"It was such a magnificent stadium and great atmosphere, we decided that we had to go again, after the tournament. And it was the same – friendly people, cheap prices, and you could drink on the terraces, and everything a bit better than in England really.

"Four of us now go over four or five times a season. If you compare it to the Premier League, it actually works out cheaper. If I wanted to go to Arsenal, say, it'd cost more than £50 a ticket, and then you have to be a member, which you pay for, and it's a complicated process.

"If you book the Channel Tunnel in advance, you can get it for £60 return for a car, the fuel is maybe £20 each, tickets are between £15 and £20 a head, and we stay in a bar where it costs £20 for a basic room. So, depending on booze, you can do it for about £80 – and you get these €1 bottles of beer which are about a litre.

"People are milling about together, drinking, having a good time – you can't be seen drinking anywhere near a Premier League game, let alone in the stands.

"We went to the German Cup final in May [2015], and one of my friends, who is now based in Qatar, travelled for it. The ticket was about £25 each – whereas the Conference Play-Off final at Wembley a couple of weeks earlier would have been £46 each after booking fees.

"There's a definite pride when one of the 'Dortmund Jung' [youngsters] plays or scores, it just means a bit more to the fans. It's a little bit different at BVB, because of the size of the club, they can afford to spend on bigger players from other areas, but if you look at many German clubs, teams like Freiburg rely entirely on their academy players – they'll never spend more than €200,000 on a player, because they don't have to."

Another British man to identify himself as a Dortmund fan is Ben McFadyean, 45, from Fulham, West London, who started to follow the club at a young age, as his stepfather came from the area. Since 1984, he has been closely involved with the club, and runs the official Borussia Dortmund Fan Club London group, for the burgeoning number of BVB fans based in the English capital.

The supporter club's final meeting of the 2014/15 season was for the DFB Pokal final defeat against Wolfsburg. Hundreds of Dortmund fans came together to watch the match in a German gastropub in Central London, with a sea of yellow forming outside the premises, echoing the scenes being played out around the actual venue for the final, some 700 miles away in Berlin. For those who happened to be passing, you might have assumed it was an English team being passionately cheered on.

91

Chapter 8

Ben explains: "We organise Public Viewing Parties for fans. So, if there's a big Champions League game on at Arsenal, we'll hire a warehouse near the Emirates, and everyone who hasn't got a ticket for the game can watch it together there rather than alone in a pub somewhere.

"German football is about respect and mutual understanding and supporting each other. We are a black and yellow army, we are friends, and we want to help each other out if another is in need. So those who travel to London without a ticket can have somewhere to come to watch the game, with a cheap beer, and be with fellow fans.

"That's the whole ethos of Dortmund, it's about mutuality, and it's the difference between the Bundesliga and the Premier League. Dortmund respects the loyalty and commitment of their fans – what you put in is what you get back.

"If you look at Jock Stein's tomb, it says 'football without the fans is nothing', and that's the truth. When you realise that, like the Bundesliga has, it gives you a new perspective. Dortmund know that they wouldn't be anything without the Südtribüne – their fans are truly the 12th man.

"I remember going to game in the Eighties, when they were rubbish, and were fighting relegation. The stadium was practically empty. Now, they sell out 84,000 seats every week. Why? Because the club has invested in the fans. They keep prices low and there's even an entire department dedicated to the fans' needs. Not only do supporters own shares in the club, but they get to vote on issues, too.

"I don't think it's impossible for an English club to do the same, it's just that they'd need to change their attitude and it'll take time. At the moment, there's so much exploitation in the Premier League, and fans don't want that.

"People got involved with the fan club primarily because of the 2006 World Cup, they've seen how amazing German football really is, and because they are very disillusioned and saddened by the state of English football and the national team itself.

"So, in a multimedia and multicultural world, they've found that it's just as easy to support the New York Yankees or Borussia Dortmund as it is to follow Oxford United or Arsenal.

"In fact, it's often easier. I actually proved, in a documentary for *Sky*, that it is cheaper to go and watch German football as an English fan, than it is the Premier League. A group of us went to Dortmund one weekend, and then to Arsenal another, and it worked out more cost effective to travel to Germany for a game.

"For me, the rise of German football is the other side of the coin of globalisation, where the Premier League became popular in Asia and Africa. In just the same way, the Bundesliga has become popular in the UK."

Ben's fan club has contemporaries around Britain for Bayern Munich, Schalke and Hamburg online. The founders of the HSV supporters UK group write on their website, by way of introduction: "The [club] was founded in 2004 by 3 HSV fans from Blackburn, Lancashire… Ruth Curtis is a life-long Manchester City fan who has followed HSV since visiting the Imtech Arena for a pre-season match between City and HSV in 2002.

"Jim Curtis has been a HSV fan since 2002. He had a season ticket for Manchester City for 20+ years in the days when you could afford to have one without having to live off bread and water. He now has a season ticket for his local club Accrington Stanley and is also involved in Chester FC.

"Dave "Kaiser" Pearson has been a HSV fan since 1998. He has followed Glasgow Rangers for many years and can remember their glory years in Europe. He is also involved in the Linfield North of England Supporters Club which backs the Linfield club in Belfast."

These founders, it is fair to say, are 'proper' football people – their involvement isn't for the success or glamour, but for the truest elements of support: a sense of belonging, feeling valued, and being able to have an impact. Their continued involvement in smaller sides in Britain reflects that – and shows that, despite the size of Bundesliga giants like Hamburg, their approach to fans hasn't been sacrificed.

Another German side who have developed a cult following in the UK – and indeed the world – despite none of the recent success and silverware that Dortmund have had to promote their philosophies, is second tier outfit St Pauli. The club have never won a major honour, and only avoided relegation to the third division by a single point in the 2014/15 campaign, but St Pauli boast a unique appeal.

It's something that inspired Sussex born John Baine, 57 – better known as punk poet and musician Attila the Stockbroker. A Brighton supporter – he was at the forefront of the 15-year campaign to save his team from extinction, and worked as a stadium announcer for 14 years – he explains his affections for the small club from Hamburg.

"In the mid-1980s I was starting to get loads of offers to tour overseas. As you'd expect, a lot of West German leftist activists and organisers had come to the shows in East Germany, especially East Berlin: I got offers to play in West Germany and took them up with gusto.

"At a big left wing festival in the Ruhr in 1988 I was approached by a pissed bloke in a strange looking brown football strip.

"I joined him for yet another beer and he told me a story. A story of how, in the early 80s, squatters had started to move into Hafenstrasse in the central dock area of St Pauli in the great port city of Hamburg and how, around 1986, football fans among the squatters had begun to watch matches at St Pauli, a little community club not far away which, up until that point, had just a few thousand supporters.

"One of the squatters, Volker Ippig, was given a goalkeeping trial – he was taken on by the club and a legend was born. Left wing football fans from all over Hamburg – many of them HSV supporters disillusioned by the violence and racism prevalent there – started going to St Pauli, joined by more and more people from the local scene, and in a year or so attendances had quadrupled, many of the newcomers committed anti fascists and punks.

"Right up my street, of course, and I resolved to visit as soon as I could. It took me a year or so to get my first gig in Hamburg coordinated so I could get to a St Pauli match.

"I can still remember the feeling of that initial game, of meeting leading activist Sven Brux in the squatted hairdressers at Beim Grunen Jager which had been turned into the first alternative club shop and of being in a lovely old stand (the Gegengerade) full of people who shared my politics, my musical tastes and my love of beer.

"It was brilliant - and I have been back to St Pauli many, many times since, while on tour in Germany.

"Over 25 years I have seen the club grow from a local rallying point for disaffected punk rock football fans into a truly global phenomenon and have done countless gigs there, both pub shows organised by fans, and official events hosted by the club itself in the larger Hamburg venues, Markthalle and Docks.

"I'm Brighton till I die, but St Pauli will always have a place in my heart."

St Pauli's popularity in the UK is almost on a par with Dortmund, with at least five different supporter clubs set up for fans in different British regions. But it's not just the English Premier League that is leaving British supporters feeling disenfranchised. Another supporter to hold dual allegiances is Edinburgh-based Celtic fan, George Docherty, 47, who actually developed a fondness for Dortmund while on duty with the Bhoys.

He recalls: "I first went to Germany in 1987, when Celtic were playing Dortmund in the UEFA Cup. Through that trip, I met a Scottish guy who lived there, a fellow Celtic fan, and we kept in touch – I'd go to visit him from time to time.

"By 1992, I'd become a Dortmund fan. We went over again with Celtic, and the reception we received from the city as a whole was exceptional – there was a great atmosphere between the fans.

"They put on a massive 'fantreffen', a huge fan meeting in the centre of the town, and it was an absolutely fantastic thing to experience, something I'd never experienced at an away game anywhere.

"So I started following them then, from afar, watching them whenever they were on the TV, though the coverage wasn't as good then.

"I used to have Sky Sports, but it was just English Premier League all the time – and a little bit of this wee league here and there. But BT Sport now show the Scottish Premiership and the Bundesliga, which shows how far the league's popularity has come.

"One day, I found a Facebook page for Edinburgh Borussen, and I couldn't believe it – I'd thought I was the only one here – so I signed up. I got in contact, and met up with one of the lads the following

Saturday for the Dortmund game. Now, we do that regularly – and there's a pub ten minutes up the road from me that shows the Dortmund games.

"We get fans from Germany coming over quite a lot, and turning up in the pub, and meeting us that way, through the club. There's a real social attitude for German fans.

"If you go to a game in Germany, you see how much they do it right. Here, in Scotland, the fans are shepherded, especially the away fans, to the ground, with the police keeping you all apart. There's no community feel to it.

"But, in Dortmund, it's totally different. It's the small things that count there – if you've got a match ticket there that doubles up as your transport ticket for the day. That sort of thing makes it.

"You're not treated like sheep, but as human beings, which is reflected in the attendances. You rarely see an empty seat in a Bundesliga game, even if it's just a mid-table match with nothing riding on it.

"Stadiums there have four sides – we have some in Scotland with only two, which is embarrassing – it's just all properly done.

"Every time we go over, we always end up meeting up with the guys we've met on previous trips, it's just a big party and it's great fun. There's no politics, no religion – although Dortmund is a kind of religion for fans – which is a refreshing change from following Celtic over the years, where I've experienced all sorts of nonsense.

"On a Saturday, if I'm not working, and I have the choice between going to a Celtic game at home, or watching Dortmund at the Brauhaus, I'll chose the pub every time."

And it's not just British fans who have found themselves paying more attention to the German game – our clubs have been casting admiring glances at the Bundesliga, too.

When Jürgen Klopp, a cult figure at Dortmund for the success and ethos he helped to build at the club, announced his departure for the end of the 2014/15 season, many English clubs would have sat up and taken notice.

Manchester City were linked with a swoop to replace the out of favour Manuel Pellegrini, though they wouldn't match Klopp's club requirements, and some Arsenal fans were calling for their side to do the same with Arsène Wenger – despite a second successive FA Cup success.

West Ham tried, and failed, to launch an ambitious coup for 'Kloppo', as he became affectionately known at Dortmund, while Liverpool owners are said to have agonised over whether he should replace Brendan Rodgers after a disappointing season at Anfield – an arena the German would relish.

*

It wasn't so long ago that the sight of a German footballer playing in England would be considered something of a rarity – Matthias Breitkreutz was the first of the Premier League era, making his Aston Villa debut in 1992, but he only managed a bit-part role during his time at the club, while former Liverpool and Man City midfielder Didi Hamann made the most appearances of his compatriots with 268 games.

But players like Hamann, until recently, have proved the exception – only 40 Germans had played in the Premier League by the summer of 2014, with just eight of them managing more than 100 league games. Felix Magath's ill-fated seven-month spell at Fulham, meanwhile, remains the only time a German manager has been employed by a Premier League club.

However, in recent years, there's been something of a German revolution within English football as well as their own – as an increasing number appear, and make more of a mark than ever before.

Indicative of this trend was Mesut Özil becoming Arsenal's club record signing in the summer of 2013, with Arsène Wenger bucking his previous trend for conservative signings by splurging £42.5million on the playmaker. In North London, Özil joined Lukas Podolksi, Serge Gnarby and Per Mertesacker as a German Gunner, following in the footsteps of Jens Lehmann's successful stint at the Emirates.

Summer 2014 saw another German name arrive in England, with promising midfielder Emre Can joining Liverpool from Leverkusen— and, though he was mostly used as makeshift defender, the Bayern Munich youth graduate was one of the few new arrivals to impress at Anfield. His move to the Premier League was significant because Bayern had retained a buy-back clause when selling him to Leverkusen, and Can had earned comparisons to the likes of Bastian Schweinsteiger and Michael Ballack.

A year later, Liverpool revisited the Bundesliga, splurging £29million on Hoffenheim forward Roberto Firmino, making the Brazil star their second most expensive player in history – their scouts suitably impressed by his performances in Germany.

Elsewhere, Stoke landed defender Philipp Wollscheid from Leverkusen, Manchester United landed national team captain Schweinsteiger in a much-lauded move, while Tottenham swooped within days of the season ending to sign Cologne's Austrian defender Kevin Wimmer.

Even champions Chelsea have dabbled in the German market. They signed winger André Schürrle in 2013 for £18million, and he helped them to the title in the 2014/15 season, though he returned to Germany in the January transfer window, with a move to Wolfsburg. Blues boss Jose Mourinho also dispatched three young talents – Thorgan Hazard, Oriol Romeu, and Tomáš Kalas – on loan to the Bundesliga, showing his faith in the league as a testing ground for future stars, or at least as a platform to sell on his surplus. The Special One's biggest German signing for the West London club, of course, was Michael Ballack in 2006, the midfield titan enjoying a trophy-laden four years at Stamford Bridge.

Overseas, Real Madrid's annual summer splurge included the £21million capture of Toni Kroos, four days after he'd lifted the 2014 World Cup with Germany. That made him the ninth German Madrista, following the likes of Christoph Metzelder, Özil, and Sami Khedira in more recent history. Title rivals Barcelona were also busy plundering the Bundesliga, announcing the capture of Mönchengladbach goalkeeper Marc-André ter Stegen for £9.7million

– becoming the club's cup keeper as they went on to complete a treble. A third German landed in Spain when Valencia signed defender Shkodran Mustafi – part of the World Cup squad – for £5.7million from Sampdoria, having previously spent three years with Everton as a teenager.

In Italy, Fiorentina spent around £14million on Germany striker Mario Gomez in 2013, while attacking counterpart Miroslav Klose has led the line for Lazio since 2011. But the passage of talent has mostly been from Italy to Germany in recent years. Bayern pounced for Roma's much-admired defender Medhi Benatia ahead of the 2014/15 season, parting with £19million to land him, as Dortmund snatched Serie A top scorer Ciro Immobile from Torino, while promising defender Tin Jedvaj completed a move from Roma to Leverkusen.

During the 2013/14 season, 292 German players plied their trade in the big five leagues, earning an average of £1,341,590 a year – making them the 26th highest ranked nationality in terms of pay, according to Sporting Intelligence's *Global Sports Salaries Survey*. Taking out small sample sizes, that means they trail only English (£2.09million) and Brazilian (£1.76million) players in terms of the best-paid nationalities – their star very much on the rise. The average Italian player in the big five leagues, for instance, earns £956,612 a year; his French equivalent £1.01million; and their Spanish teammate £1.16million. The highest paid nation on the list is Belgium, with an average of £2.16million, although that figure is inflated by the fact that there are only 34 Belgians operating across the relevant leagues. Which perhaps also explains why Montenegro are second in the rankings.

The popularity of German players is also demonstrated by the fact that they are the third best-represented nation across the big five leagues, trailing only Spain (398) and France (388). Although, it'll cost you a fair whack to sign a German superstar – at the 2014 World Cup, Germany's squad was the second best paid, averaging £3.86million a year, behind only Spain, whose typical player earned £4.11million in that time. Third on the list, of course, was England, with an average annual salary of £3.5million.

*

Teutophile attitudes have also spread to our televisions, with BT Sport extending their Bundesliga rights until 2017, offering viewers in the UK and Ireland 115 live matches a season from September 2015. That's an increase of 15 matches per season on the previous deal, which they picked up when buying ESPN out of various UK football contracts. The channel also airs games from the DFL Supercup, plus preview and highlight shows. It's given the full treatment, in short. And the audience has reacted – with viewing figures up 70 per cent for the 2014/15 season, compared with the previous campaign.

Speaking of the deal, Head of BT Sport, Simon Green, said: "I am delighted that the Bundesliga recognised that BT Sport has made a big commitment to German football and will continue to promote and foster the league for UK sports lovers in the future."

Jörg Daubitzer, managing director of DFL Sports Enterprises – aka the commercial department for German football – said: "Never before have so many Bundesliga matches been shown with such broad penetration in the United Kingdom. We are very pleased to be able to continue this successful cooperation."

And well he might be pleased – the extension of the deal with BT Sport was part of a marketing push that has more than doubled the league's income in foreign TV rights from €70million to over €150million. In November 2014, nine months after announcing the renewal with BT, DFL Sports Enterprises awarded audio-visual media rights to a further 18 countries or regions for the 2015/2016 and 2016/2017 Bundesliga seasons: Armenia, Azerbaijan, Belarus, Cyprus, Georgia, Greece, Kazakhstan, Kyrgyzstan, Malta, Moldova, Russia, Spain (including Andorra), Tajikistan, Turkey, Turkmenistan, Uzbekistan and Ukraine.

Also beginning in the 2015/16 season, a deal with 21st Century Fox will see the worldwide network become the 'home' of Bundesliga action throughout the Americas and in large parts of Asia for five seasons. It's a huge deal that pitches the league into direct competition with the Premier League, and with a product that is certainly comparable. In the words of Fox, the deal will "bolster the Bundesliga brand in every corner of the globe".

It's an idea that even the players are subscribing to – with an awareness that the league needs to prosper generally if specific clubs are to develop. Amongst the players interviewed for this book was Rob-Robert Zieler, part of the World Cup winning squad in 2014. When asked what Germany could learn from England, he didn't hesitate to answer – the commercial side of things is where the Premier League excels.

He said: "The marketing worldwide of the English Premier League is fantastic, the Bundesliga has the potential to be up there also, and it has caught up a lot, but the Premier League is still a step ahead. Germany is second at the moment, but we are being shown in new areas next season, which is a really good first step for the Bundesliga – but England have been doing this for the last ten years, so they will still be ahead. But I hope it works well for our league."

And he is right – Germany still trail in the wake of England commercially, but are catching up fast. DFL Sports Enterprises was only established in September 2008, and have been trailing in the Premier League's wake ever since – but, in a 10-year plan of their own, it appears that they're almost level with the market leader. And Bundesliga clubs, just like those in the English top flight, could be set for a windfall that propels them forward in terms of both reputation and finance.

For one club in particular, that could establish them as the biggest outfit not just in Germany, but in world football – something they are already mightily close to being…

Chapter 9
Bayern mighty: The global footballing colossus with a conscience. Kinda.

Not many teams can genuinely stake a claim to being the 'biggest club in the world'. La Liga's twin forces of Barcelona and Real Madrid have a justifiable shout, as do the Premier League's most successful outfit Manchester United. The fourth and final club in the mix are Bayern Munich – the dominant power in Bundesliga history and, no doubt, future. And, if the league continues to thrive as seems likely, the team once known as FC Hollywood might well become the headline act across the footballing world.

Certainly, that is already true in Germany. Bayern's vast financial superiority and the all-star cast of their first team – at the 2014 World Cup, they provided more players than any other club side, with 15 of their stars called up for international duty – has meant that they are perennial favourites for the title. Anything other than first place is an utter shock for Munich.

The gap is illustrated most clearly by a comparison of the Bundesliga's big three – although that could quite comfortably be reduced to 'one' – in Forbes' 2015 list of football's most valuable clubs. Comparing the value, revenues, debt, and increase/decrease between Bayern, Dortmund and Schalke – there is one, very clear, winner.

Forbes rank	Team	Current value	Annual change	Debt / Value	Revenue	Operating income
4	Bayern	$2.34bn	+27%	0	$661m	$78m
11	Dortmund	$700m	+17%	6%	$355m	$55m
14	Schalke	$572m	-1%	0	$290m	$57m

One horse races are a rarity in football – though having divisions topped by the same cluster of super clubs isn't – but Germany, for all of its positives and successes, might just be the closest we get in the Big Five, with only PSG's recent stranglehold in France remotely comparable.

Since 1999, Bayern have won the Bundesliga 11 times in 17 years – the only team to win the title more than once in that time were Dortmund, lifting the Bundesliga in 2002, 2011 and 2012. It is domination that makes Manchester United's Premier League era appear unpredictable. Since the Bundesliga's inauguration in 1963, Munich have lifted the league title 24 times. The next best record is the five titles that Borussia Monchengladbach and Dortmund have each claimed. Bayern have also won the German Cup six times in the last 11 years (up until 2014/15), and have reached the last four of the Champions League five times out of six since 2009.

Such is the ease with which they win their domestic league – wrapping up the 2013/14 title in March, with a record seven games to go, and ultimately finishing 19 points clear of Dortmund – that forward Thomas Muller cheekily remarked that winning in training is often more difficult than it is in league games. Though his tongue will have been firmly in his cheek, Muller's comments are quite believable – and not particularly surprising when you consider the hold Bayern possess over their rivals. Seven of the ten most expensive Bundesliga transfers of all time have been Bayern signings.

Bayern's average salary is almost double that of Dortmund, who have increasingly served as something of an unofficial – and certainly unintentional – feeder club to their rivals in recent years. Schalke, the third 'big boy' of the Bundesliga, are financially backed by Gazprom, and certainly aren't shy of investing in their playing staff – boasting the second highest wage bill in the country – but are left similarly trailing in the wake of Bayern's budget.

Munich pay the seventh highest wages in world sport, with the average weekly pay of their first team squad at £85,935. That puts them above Chelsea (£83,713 average) and Arsenal (£77,963 average) in the *Global Sports Salaries* survey by Sporting Intelligence. But they also trail the best-paying sports team in the world, France's PSG, who dish out £101,898 a week on average to their players. Second are La Liga's Real Madrid (£96,933), narrowly ahead of Man City (£96,445) and Barcelona (£90,675). The baseball team, the LA Dodgers, in fifth, are the highest non-football side in the rankings, ahead of Manchester United (£89,988 average) in sixth.

Bayern, ever the exception in their own country, are the only German team in the survey's top fifty clubs – their next highest compatriot for 2013/14 was Schalke, in 53rd, whose average first team wage was £47,878. By contrast, there are four Premier League teams in the top ten – and six in the top fifty.

It's in player salaries that Bayern really exert their strength over divisional rivals, nay, counterparts: the average first-teamer at Bayern makes £4.4million a year – two million more than their equivalents at Schalke. The third-highest payers – Dortmund – pay, on average, £2.34million a year, which is £45,093 a week, whilst the next highest club, Wolfsburg in fourth, only pay out around a third of what Bayern do. Their average first team wage is £1.59million a year, or £30,691 a week. And, below them, the numbers involved drop off dramatically. The lowest paying Premier League club during the 2013/14 season, Crystal Palace, paid a higher average wage (£19,205) than eight Bundesliga clubs.

Average Bundesliga wages, 2013/14

Rank	Team	Average wage, weekly	Average wage, annual
1	Bayern Munich	£85,953	£4,468,643
2	Schalke	£47,878	£2,489,672
3	Borussia Dortmund	£45,093	£2,344,823
4	Wolfsburg	£30,691	£1,595,944
5	Bayer Leverkusen	£29,464	£1,532,106

Rank	Team	Average wage, weekly	Average wage, annual
6	Hamburg	£25,167	£1,308,674
7	Stuttgart	£24,553	£1,276,755
8	Werder Bremen	£21,484	£1,117,161
9	Borussia Monchengladbach	£21,177	£1,101,201
10	Hannover 96	£20,256	£1,053,323
11	Hoffenheim	£19,028	£989,485
12	Eintracht Frankfurt	£18,415	£957,566
13	Nuremberg	£14,732	£766,055
14	Mainz	£14,732	£766,053
15	Hertha Berlin	£14,118	£734,134
16	Augsburg	£10,435	£542,621
17	Freiburg	£9,883	£513,894
18	Eintract Braunschweig	£9,207	£478,783

It's this disparity in wage bills that has caused some tension between Bayern and Dortmund. BVB's CEO Hans-Joachim Watzke has claimed that: "Bayern Munich want to destroy us" when discussing the ill feeling developed towards the Champions over their 'poaching' tactics. A war of words between the clubs was started by Mario Götze's controversial £31.5million move from Dortmund to Munich in 2013, then exacerbated by Robert Lewandowski's decision to follow suit a year later on a Bosman free, before being antagonised even further by Bayern's public pursuit of Marco Reus during the 2014/15 season. The traditional pre-match lunch between club bosses was scrapped as a result of the latter battle.

An exasperated Watzke spelt out his and Dortmund's grievances with Bayern quite openly, saying: "They have helped themselves to our players so we wouldn't be a danger. There are players here, at Dortmund, who are happy to play for 20% less money – but that's not the case when we're talking about 50% less money. It's like they want all of our players."

A supposedly bemused Karl-Heinz Rummenigge, Watzke's equivalent at Bayern, responded by saying his team were entitled to try and sign whomever they wanted: "We don't have to weaken anybody. Every transfer has exclusively one goal – to strengthen the team's quality."

It's a feud that has developed recently – before which the two teams shared a good relationship – with both sides holding grudges. While Dortmund resent Bayern's transfer policy, Bayern themselves weren't overly enamoured by the nature of Dortmund's exuberant celebrations when winning back-to-back titles, with thinly veiled digs targeting Munich. This was underlined by the reaction of Jürgen Klopp and his team when they beat their rivals 5-2 in the German Cup final of 2012 – the humiliation and perceived disrespect Bayern experienced was motivation for them to invest heavily in their squad, to ensure their noses wouldn't be rubbed in it again.

That 2011/12 campaign saw Bayern finish as runners-up in the Cup, Bundesliga, and Champions League, something they had no intention of repeating. Dortmund's dominance – and alleged smugness – prompted Munich to break the German transfer record, spending €40million on Athletic Bilbao midfielder Javi Martinez, while also splashing out on Mario Mandzukic (€13million), Xherdan Shaqiri (€11.5million), and mainstay defender Dante (€4.7million). They ended the campaign with four trophies – becoming the first German side to win the treble, to which they added the season opening Supercup – and by seeing off Dortmund in the Champions League final, having controversially announced the signing of their star man, Götze, a month earlier. Now, it was Bayern applying salt to the wounds.

But, if Dortmund's anger at Bayern's awkward knack of poaching their best players is understandable, their view that Munich's dominance is bad for the German games isn't necessarily a universally accepted truth.

Despite their dramatically superior financial power, regular monopoly on domestic silverware, and status as the polar opposite of an underdog, there are many people in Germany that root for Munich when it comes to European matters. With the hopes of the nation generally hung on Bayern in the Champions League, it's almost as though the Bavarians *are* Germany, and represent the Bundesliga in continental clashes. In England, domestic rivalries are such that a Chelsea fan, say, would seriously struggle to find it within themselves to cheer Manchester City on in a big European game. Normally, the opposite is true.

Chapter 9

It's a surprise revelation made by former Germany and Leverkusen defender Jens Nowotny, after I ask him if Bayern are bad for the Bundesliga. He said: "In Bayern Munich, we have a team in Germany that will not be satisfied with the Champions League semi-final, they want to go for the cup. So they'll invest more money to build a team to go for it. In Germany, if they win four of the next five titles, nobody cares about it.

"The Champions League is their goal and focus, and the Federation sees it as a good thing for the whole league. It drives them forward – it means people won't lie back and be satisfied with the situation as it is. For Germany, it's best that we have one club like Bayern Munich, which is so strong and has so much money that it can challenge for the Champions League.

"In 2015/16, we have Wolfsburg, Borussia Monchengladbach and Leverkusen in the competition. If Bayern Munich go through, no one will be surprised. If the other three get knocked out, people might say German football is so bad – only one team showed up. But we don't care about this – that one team might win the title.

"In the Champions League, Bayern Munich almost *are* Germany. When they played Barcelona in the semi-final last season, I was watching with some ex-national players – and everyone from Bremen, Leverkusen, Gladbach, all over the league, and everybody was supporting Bayern Munich, because they want a German soccer team to win in Europe.

"We are proud of that one team, and most owners of German clubs are behind Bayern Munich in the Champions League."

That support may have been fostered as Bayern aren't nearly as dominant in Europe. Though they are five times champions of the continent, three of those were in succession in the Seventies. Their fourth crown arrived after a 25-year wait in 2001, before another period of not really featuring as contenders. That changed in 2010, when Arjen Robben inspired Bayern to the final where they lost to Inter Milan, again finishing as runners up two years later with Chelsea their conquerors. The pain of two final defeats in three years was compensated for by lifting the trophy in 2013, with success over Dortmund in the final especially sweet, but the 7-0 aggregate defeat of Barcelona in the semi-finals was the definite highlight – sweeping away Europe's most lauded team brilliantly.

Bayern's swashbuckling style won them new admirers and plaudits from across the globe – and, ultimately, attracted the most sought after coach in world football, Pep Guardiola, to take charge a month later. His mission: to cement Bayern's position alongside former club Barca as Europe's leading light.

Guardiola's arrival added an air of artistry about Bayern's style – as well as a crowd of fellow Spaniards – with big name signings serving as a statement of intent. Beating Manchester United to the €20million capture of Thiago was considered a coup, and Medhi Benatio's €26million arrival came in spite of interest from Barcelona, Real Madrid, Man City and Chelsea. Almost immediately, Guardiola's appointment elevated Bayern's status from global giant to bona fide super club.

But his masterplan wasn't simply to go all 'Harlem Globetrotters' on us – Bayern's strong home-grown core has remained, and continues to serve as a point of endearment for German neutrals. Amid the expensively assembled squad Guardiola presides over, are four players who have come through the Bayern youth system and established themselves as first team regulars – captain Philipp Lahm, who was signed up by their vast scouting network aged 11; Thomas Muller arriving at 10, Holger Badstuber at 13, and Austrian David Alaba at 16. Bastian Schweinsteiger, who joined the club aged 14, was also a part of that group until he left for Manchester United in the summer of 2015.

Furthermore, the squad contains national team mainstays Manuel Neuer, Jérôme Boateng and Mario Götze, while Pep has had an eye on the next generation – promoting youth product Gianluca Gaudino to the first team for the 2014/15 campaign, where the 18-year-old became the club's fourth-youngest debutant, making 11 first team appearances. This continued development of talent wins the club plenty of fans in Germany – because if a player is good enough to be a Bayern regular, he'll almost certainly do the same for the national team.

Another to come through the ranks at Bayern, Owen Hargreaves, although he went on to represent England internationally, reinforced this attitude when making a BT Sport documentary, *Inside Bayern Munich*, about the club and what makes it unique.

Thinking back to his time in Munich, the midfielder reflected: "I came here as a young boy at 16, and to see the way the club has developed, all these people that have a connection to the club, keeping it a very family based club, I think now you have the best generation with Bastian Schweinsteiger and Philipp Lahm and it's great to see that the connection is still so important.

"I remember my first league title, we'd won the Bundesliga and we'd won the Champions League title, and we got convertibles all the way from the airport and we drove really slowly through the centre of Munich and there was a million people on the streets.

"Another one of those things which makes Bayern so special, I don't think teams celebrate as nicely as Bayern. You think about all those massive beer things which they used to pour; I think when I was in England they used to ask me about that… these little traditions are so unique.

Hargreaves spent a decade with Munich, developing into a pivotal part of the starting eleven, winning four league titles and the 2001 Champions League, before leaving for Manchester United in 2007, for a fee of £17million. But it wasn't always a given that he was going to be a popular figure in the Bayern dressing room, having arrived as a 16-year-old Canadian outsider, alone in a new country.

"When I came over, they said 'why is a Canadian kid here?'. Now, everything is far more accommodating for the young guys and everybody's really helpful, whereas when I came through it was really rough and tumble. I had a lot of fights in my first year and I'm a very quiet and respectful guy but on the pitch it was a battle.

"(Stefan) Effenberg was the leader of the pack and he was tough too because he was very demanding and very physical. I remember he used to kick me all the time and then help me back up. But that's part of the school, that's how it was.

"I remember we had a friendly, in Tunisia I think, and I was about to board the plane and I said 'here Effy, you go first'. Then after about a year he said 'you get on first, you're going to be my successor anyway'. And that's how it was, you had to prove over time that you were worthy in a way.

"That was the old mentality, the German mentality of fight and work. One of the most important things for young players is to work. It was aggressive, it was hostile at times, but that's the nature of sport, the survival of the fittest. It's not like that anymore, now the leaders are Philipp and Bast, who are far more accommodating and helpful."

That Hargreaves, who now works as a pundit on BT Sport, often covering the German league, was able to make a documentary about his former club for an English audience is testament to just how popular Bayern and the Bundesliga have become over the last five years. Winning an unprecedented treble and appointing Pep Guardiola in 2013 might have been the tipping point but, by the end of the next season, when Germany lifted the World Cup, the groundswell of plaudits for German football had been established as fact.

One person who is a bit miffed by the hipster hyperbole suddenly lavishing the German game with praise – this book included, no doubt – is former Bayern Munich forward Alan McInally, who says that the now acclaimed approaches have always been the same in the Bundesliga, dating back to the late Eighties, when he had his four-year stint in Bavaria. Coming from the English First Division, better known then for crowd trouble, the Scottish forward was impressed with what he saw. The now Sky Sports pundit reflected: "The fan focus has always been in place in Germany, not just part of this 10-year plan.

"There was one thing that really opened my eyes during my time at Munich. They had a Tür der offenen tag – an open door day – and there were 35,000 people at the training ground. I got into training and I thought there was a game on and I'd arrived late – I thought 'are we playing here today?' But it was just so fans could watch us train. There were a couple of Astro Turf pitches next to where we used to train, and they put up a massive beer tent, that covered the whole of the football pitch.

"It wasn't just like get a burger and a hot dog, and you might get a beer, this thing was massive, and everything was free. It was absolutely unbelievable. If that's not making the fans feel included and valued, I don't know what is.

"So, in that sense, I saw a difference in their attitude towards the fans. And I think that, when you speak about the German model, they certainly have the fans in mind when they think about a lot of things.

"I'm not saying the English game doesn't, but there just seems to be more opportunities for the 'common man', as it were, to go and watch football in the Bundesliga, and they've got it right. The model is spot on at the moment."

That approach wasn't the only area where McIlnally registered an improvement – away from the drinking culture rife in the English top-flight, he discovered a more professional and informed lifestyle adopted by the German stars.

"It was a huge culture shock for me when I joined Bayern Munich. To be fair, at Aston Villa before I went to Germany, Graham Taylor was the manager at the time, and he was pretty strict and preparation was good – but it was a step up when I went to the Bundesliga.

"That was in terms of the way they trained, the hours they trained. It wasn't just once a day. You could be in Monday afternoon, Tuesday afternoon, and twice on the Wednesday too. But the recovery was as big as training itself on the continent. Things like that were different.

"Jupp Heynckes was the coach at the time, and I had to get used to the way German football was run, and Bayern played.

"They've always had better preparation for games in Germany, by the players as well as the staff. Over the last ten years, English players have caught up a bit – in terms of being a bit more professional. They're up to speed now with the way things have been happening in Germany since time began.

"And that's why they had been more successful in Europe, why they had been more successful in tournaments. That was the biggest thing, their attention to detail and the way that people prepared for games – it was more professional, to an extent."

That attention to detail extends to the club's marketing department and focus – which is probably the Bundesliga's closest equivalent to the Premier League. Sponsorship wise, their commercial partnerships are second only to Manchester United, and worth more than twice that of Real Madrid's agreements.

The Allianz Arena, to some controversy initially, is home to 2,000 Arsenal-style business club seats, plus 106 boxes charging sponsors from €100,000 a year to hire – the biggest costing €350,000. There are also eight 'event' boxes for hire, and the stadium is in regular use on non-match days with sponsor events and corporate hospitality.

For the 2015/16 season, Bayern's tie-ups were worth a mammoth $143million – a huge income for any top-level club, and a significant advantage over their domestic rivals. With the likes of Barcelona ($80million) and Manchester City ($79million) trailing in their wake, it's also a key way of bridging the gap between them and their continental counterparts, who can boast preferential TV deals. By comparison, Juventus, who reached the 2015 Champions League final, generated $45million in sponsorship during the 15/16 campaign.

Biggest European sponsorship deals, 2015/16 season

Club	Kit	Jersey	Stadium	Total
Manchester United	Adidas, $114million	Chevrolet, $80million	Aon (training ground/kit) $24million	$218million
Bayern Munich	Adidas, $100million	Deutsche Telekom, $34million	Allianz, $9million	$143million
Chelsea	Adidas, $44million	Yokohama Rubber, $60million	None	$104million
Barcelona	Nike, $39million	Qatar Sports Investment and Intel, $41million	None	$80million
Arsenal	Puma, $34million	Emirates, $46million	Combined with jersey	$80million

Club	Kit	Jersey	Stadium	Total
Manchester City	Nike, $18million	Etihad Airways, $61million	Combined with jersey	$79million
Real Madrid	Adidas, $36million	Emirates, $34million	None	$70million
Liverpool	Warrior, $38million	Standard Chartered, $30million	None	$68million
PSG	Nike, $22million	Emirates, $28million	None	$50million
Juventus	Adidas	Jeep	None	$45million

And Bayern have managed Germany's famous 50+1 ownership ruling cleverly, too. Their partnership with Allianz has proved particularly fruitful – the insurance giant parted with a substantial sum for 30 years of naming rights for the Allianz Arena, before agreeing to purchase an 8.33% stake in the club.

The latter deal wiped out all the remaining debt on the stadium, which had already been paid for mostly by the naming rights agreement, as well as funding significant investment into the club's youth and training facilities. Allianz have, effectively, paid for most of the Arena that is named after them. Alongside similar deals with fellow German superpowers Audi and Adidas, Bayern have sold a quarter of the club's shares in order to keep pace with their biggest European rivals in the transfer market. Even Dortmund President Hans-Joachim Watzke offered begrudging praise for the deal – although he did suggest that it would further broaden the gap between Bayern and teams like his.

And bullish Bayern honchos have no doubt that will be the case – as they are determined to maintain the status quo, and the club's grip on the German game. Captain Philipp Lahm, who has come to personify his club – and, indeed, national team – whenever he represents them on the pitch, is confident that Munich will continue to be a major hub in the footballing world. He said: "I'm sure that the club will continue. The structure of the club is so good – it's still a family club but, economically, the club is so stable and the club works so well. It's such a strong base that the club has to become successful.

"I'm not worried about the future. In other countries, like England, the TV money that is available, they have a big advantage financially. I think the tradition [Bayern] has, being successful for decades, is obviously very well known – in England, in Spain, in Italy. But, economically, we have a lot of financial firepower too."

And, when he eventually hangs up his boots, Lahm intends to continue the Bayern tradition of great on-field leaders recreating themselves as off-field 'captains': "I've been at Bayern Munich since I was 12-years-old. This is my home. I have a contract until 2018, I might play for fun in my free time for another team, but not in professional football. Of course I can imagine myself staying here after I've finished playing – that goes without question."

It's a path that one-time goal machine – Bayern's second most prolific forward in history, behind the great Gerd Müller – and now CEO, Karl-Heinz Rummenigge, followed after retirement. It's something, he says, that makes up part of the club's identity. "I believe fans like that and sometimes I have the impression that the other clubs are not confident to do it. I always make the example – if the sun is shining, everybody would like to get the warmth of the sun, and maybe sometimes Presidents or Germans, or whatever, are afraid that former players can get more sun than themselves.

"But I believe it is a good thing, so we have some players in our team like Manuel Neuer, Bastian Schweinsteiger, Philipp Lahm, maybe Thomas Muller, who could run that business as well in the future." It would certainly make for a decent 'vets' five-a-side team.

But having these legendary luminaries looming over the club isn't always a good thing. Just ask Louis Van Gaal about his time in Bavaria – his acrimonious and fractious relationship with then President Uli Hoeness meant that the Dutchman was dispensed with at, virtually, the first opportunity, just months after leading the club to a domestic double and Champions League final.

For Van Gaal, the power struggle undermined his authority, and hastened his departure – the similarly headstrong manager subsequently pointing out that he wasn't the only one to fall foul of Hoeness' stranglehold, as General Manager Christian Nerlinger was also sacked shortly after his own Allianz Arena departure. He raged: "The only one who kept pressing for my sacking was Uli Hoeness. I would never work with him again. He has too much power, he uses that. Even the board can't work against his opinion in the long run. I worked with Nerlinger and witnessed how much pressure he came under from Hoeness. That's why I predicted his sacking."

You can quite imagine, then, LVG revelling in the schadenfreude of Hoeness' own demise – sentenced to three and a half years in prison for tax evasion, prompting his resignation from Bayern, and a relinquishing of control that Van Gaal would have relished.

Not that Hoeness is alone in courting controversy. Former President Franz Beckenbauer – whose loose-lipped style has made him far better suited to his current career of media personality than his previous employ as Bayern administrator – was at the centre of a national storm in 2003, after suggesting that the club would join Serie A in protest at league sanctions over a controversial marketing deal.

Following a DFL investigation over a secret £14.8million top-up payment from Kirch Media – who went bust a year earlier, casting the league into temporary disarray – the possibility of a points deduction was mooted, prompting a furious backlash from Bayern. First to set the tone was Rummenigge, then club chairman, who publicly announced: "We will not accept a points deduction. That's a question of principle. If there is a verdict that we cannot accept, the consequence would be that we would pull out of all bodies [in German football]."

Beckenbauer, in his trademark style, steamed in with little subtlety: "The Bundesliga will have to see how they go without us. We'll join the league in Italy and play against Milan and Rome." Of course, that situation didn't play out – Bayern, who were 14 points clear at the time anyway, avoided a deduction, and went on to romp to the Bundesliga title.

*

It's not all bad when it comes to the Bavarian behemoth. Although their wealth, power and success has made them an easy target for envy, Bayern have often leveraged this status for the benefit of others – in particular, local rivals 1860 Munich, who have gained from the giants' generosity on numerous occasions. Whether that be through money-spinning friendlies, over-the-odds transfer fees, or direct cash injections.

In other instances, Bayern have helped clubs in dire straits, with lucrative friendly matches from which all the proceeds went to their ailing opponents; amongst the clubs to benefit from this are St Pauli; Fortuna Sittard, Bayern icon Mark van Bommel's hometown club; and Hansa Rostock in 2012, which raised around €1million for the third tier club, enough to secure their license.

An earlier Bayern intervention effectively kept rivals Dortmund afloat in 2003 and, a decade earlier, they'd done similarly for Dynamo Dresden – purchasing Alexander Zickler for 2.3million Deutschemarks, an inflated price perceived to be a way of helping the strugglers out of a financial hole.

With that in mind, plus the entire status and size of the club, just where do Bayern stand in the pantheon of European greats? Their place in history is assured, but can you definitively rank them in modern football? Well, apparently, yes – second. That's according to leading brand valuation and strategy consultancy Brand Finance, who compile the 'Football 50' list – which ranks the top fifty teams in Europe in terms of their 'brand power' and ability to monetise that.

The values are calculated using the 'royalty relief approach', which estimates future sales and the royalty rate charged by the brand – in this instance, the clubs – for that use. The seven determining factors are:

1. Calculate brand strength on a scale of 0 to 100 – this, the Brand Strength Index, measures the interest in each club, and the likelihood of converting that into a sale.

2. Calculate the three main revenue streams – broadcasting, commercial, and match day.

3. Assign a royalty rate by taking the range from the brand's sector and multiplying by the brand strength score.

4. Work out brand-specific revenues estimating a proportion of parent company revenues, which are attributable to a specific brand.

5. Estimate forecast revenues using historic revenue records, equity analyst forecasts, and economic growth rates.

6. Apply royalty rate to forecast revenues to generate brand revenues.

7. Brand revenues are discounted post tax to a net present value, which equals the brand value.

Thankfully, someone else conducts those calculations, producing an annual report of the best-rated brands in world football. Top of the list, perhaps unsurprisingly, is Manchester United – the first to hit the billion dollar mark – but Bayern aren't far behind; and, indeed, topped the same list in 2014. The gap between the Bavarians and other German sides is tell-tale of the gulf in the German game.

World's most valuable football club brands, 2015

Rank	Team	Value
1	Manchester United	$1.2billion
2	Bayern Munich	$933million
3	Real Madrid	$873million
4	Man City	$800million
5	Chelsea	$795million
6	Barcelona	$773million
7	Arsenal	$703million
8	Liverpool	$577million
9	PSG	$541million
10	Tottenham	$360million
11	Juventus	$350million
12	Dortmund	$326million
13	Schalke	$302million
14	AC Milan	$244million
15	Everton	$228million
28	Bayer Leverkusen	$135million
32	Stuttgart	$121million
36	Wolfsburg	$116million
41	Hamburg	$103million
44	Werder Bremen	$88million
45	Borussia Monchengladbach	$86million

If there is one chink in Bayern's seemingly bulletproof armour, it's that the side has an aging core of near-on irreplaceable superstars. But you can bet that, when the time comes to move them on, Munich will prioritise success over sentiment – which Schweinsteiger's shock switch to England demonstrated. As Sporting Director Matthias Sammer – a legendary member of Dortmund's alumni – explained before Schweinsteiger's departure: "There is a change of generations, not now and not tomorrow, but Bayern Munich need to be aware and conscious. Philipp (Lahm) and Basti (Schweinsteiger) are in their early thirties, Xabi Alonso is older, Arjen Robben and Franck Ribery over 30.

"If you have big players then you have to discuss with those big players these matters – as it influences the future of the club. Because, of course, you can say Philipp has until '18, Xabi Alonso and Bastian until '16 but we have to make plans as a club before it's too late. We need to intervene earlier. I am always of the mindset that these big players do not like approaching the subject and like to think that they can play on to when they're 45. But this is not the way. The club has a responsibility, it does not only entail Philipp Lahm – after Lahm the club has to continue to work. That is his duty as well as the club's duty."

Apart from winning trophies, and routing opponents, it's perhaps this no-nonsense approach that best surmises Bayern and their dominance. But, scratch below the surface of the Bundesliga's behemoth, down past Dortmund, and the league is littered with success stories. Munich's mission is becoming the best of the best, but there are plenty of examples of German football's positives provided by the best of the rest...

Chapter 10
The best of the rest

Bayern Munich and Borussia Dortmund might dominate the headlines that surround the Bundesliga, but further down the food chain there is plenty more to talk about, with many clubs prospering as part of German football's renaissance.

One of those at the forefront of the 10-year academy plan was Schalke, who will be more than a little annoyed that fierce rivals Dortmund have had so much success and praise in recent years. But, in following the same youth-focused path, there's no reason why they cannot follow suit.

In the aftermath of Euro 2000, Schalke teamed up with the Berger Feld school that is located a stone's throw from their stadium – the Veltins Arena, which was built just a year later, ahead of the 2006 World Cup, complete with retracting roof and field – to dramatically improve that standard of PE classes taught at the institution, offering youngsters top level training sessions instead.

For prodigies learning their trade at Schalke, there is a constant reminder of the club's working class roots, as the youth programme is known as the Knappenschmiede, which translates as 'forge of the miners'. It conjures an evocative image that provides plenty of perspective for the highly touted youngsters who progress through the ranks.

For Oliver Ruhnert, the Academy Director, this journey is enabled due to constant conversation between the youth team staff and the first-team equivalents. He said: "It's all about having a good strategy. Our youth department is in very close contact with the professional team.

"Together, we make plans for the coming years: what kind of players will be needed for different positions, what skills they should have, etc. Both sides trust in these agreements consistently, and that's how it works."

And work it does – with plenty of talent that keeps emerging. In recent years, their most notable graduates have been goalkeeper Manuel Neuer, who has established himself as the number one for both Bayern Munich and Germany; Moritz Volz, who was poached by Arsenal's scouting network and added to their extensive reserve roster; and future Real Madrid and Arsenal playmaker Mesut Özil.

The departure of each of these three players rankled with Schalke at the time – and, particularly in the case of Neuer and Özil, prompted a sense of 'what if' amongst their support. Özil's transfer to Werder Bremen in 2008 came at a time when he was rated as the hottest property in German football, and originated from a disagreement about money – making his exit avoidable in the eyes of the fans. Two years later, he was Germany's standout breakthrough star at the South Africa World Cup and commanding the attention of the world's biggest clubs.

If that was frustrating, the loss of Neuer was even more painful; having joined the club as a four-year-old, the sweeper keeper progressed through every age rank at Schalke before establishing himself as first choice aged just 20, later becoming captain. His decision to leave for Bayern, for a fee of €22million – which made him the second most expensive goalkeeper in history, behind Gigi Buffon – drew ire from the Schalke faithful, and initial scepticism from Bayern fans, with both sides angered at the switch between rivals. So much so, Munich had to call a meeting with supporters' representatives to ease the hostility towards Neuer. It wore off pretty swiftly though – within weeks of his arrival, he broke the club's record for the most competitive clean sheets in a row, after going more than 1,000 minutes without conceding a goal, breaking a record set by legendary predecessor Oliver Kahn.

Neuer isn't the only successful goalkeeper to emerge from Schalke's ranks – on one match day in 2012, five Bundesliga teams lined up with a man from Schalke between the sticks – Neuer for Bayern, Lars Unnerstall for Schalke, Ralf Fährmann at Frankfurt, Mohamed Amsif for Augsburg, and Patrick Rakovsky for Nürnberg. It was a significant achievement for the club's youth academy, and still proudly remembered. While, in 2015, B-team stopper Timon Wellenreuther, then 19, started their Champions League clash with

Real Madrid, the youngest ever German keeper to play in the competition.

Though the teenager's promotion was through necessity – with Schalke's two first choice keepers injured – it was hardly unusual: it is the club's stated aim to nurture at least one player from each academy age group into a full Bundesliga professional. Amongst the Germany squad that won the 2014 World Cup were four Schalke graduates – alumni Neuer and Özil, as well as the ever-present Benedikt Howedes, who joined Schalke as a 13-year-old; and the highly-touted Julian Draxler, who started at the club aged just eight and made his league debut at 16.

The latest off the production line, teenager Max Meyer, was included in Jogi Löw's provisional 30-man squad for the tournament, after being discovered by Schalke as a 14-year-old; he inherited the club's number seven shirt from legendary forward Raul just three years later.

Another graduate, Leroy Sané, turned professional in March 2014, aged 18, and became a part of the first team squad; defender Marvin Friedrich made the same progression six months later; and goalkeeper Ralf Fahrmann, who joined the club at 15, became first choice during that same season. Elsewhere, Joel Matip came through the academy and is now a Cameroon international, while Dortmund's highly rated Ilkay Gundogan also spent a year in Schalke's youth system.

It's a production line that is expected to continue yielding stars, as head of Academy Bodo Menze told the *Daily Mail* in 2013: "The development of talent has always played a role in the traditions of this club. We have teams from Under 9 to Under 23 and we select every team according to performance. The most important factors are to be fast, quick in decisions with technical skills and tactical skills – but also with strong character and an identity with the club."

That mentality is fostered by inspirational imagery that lines the corridors of the main entrance to the Veltins Arena – with talents chosen to attend the club's own school literally looking up to legends of Schalke's past, including Ernst Kuzorra, Fritz Szepan, Willi Koslowski, and Manfred Kreuz. The grainy photos of players from long ago eras serve to highlight the legacy on offer to those who make an impact on the club.

And Menze clearly thinks that there is a crop of current internationals who could be remembered similarly: "Julian Draxler was always a great footballer, always with his own interpretation and opinion of the game. There were doubts about Manuel Neuer at the age of 16, but the year after he grew something like 20 centimetres and managed to find his way and his qualities.

"With Benni Howedes, I recognized at Under 15 level he was not very eye-catching, but he had such a low error rate and always played very clean and safe and you have to look very hard to see such players. With Mesut Özil, it was the contrary, he was the classic number ten. He fascinated from the beginning and was an extraordinary player on the pitch at Under 17 level.

"We can't make the mistake of easing up. In success, one makes the biggest errors."

This proven track record of developing their own stars is probably a large part of Schalke's appeal – with membership levels rocketing in recent years, climbing from 10,000 in 1991 to around 130,000 in 2014. That makes them the second-biggest sports club in Germany, behind Bayern, and third biggest in the world – with Benfica top of that list. Interestingly, a breakdown of the Schalke membership range in 2014 revealed that 20% were female, while 14% were under the age of ten.

This, too, is a source of pride at Schalke, Ruhnert explained: "Schalke is a very traditional club and our supporters are very important – the basis, so to say. Therefore, we have public training sessions almost every day and a great party at the beginning of each season to guarantee a good contact between fans and players.

"Additionally, our club has an annual general meeting where club members have the possibility to vote about several topics. They are part of the 'Schalke family'."

*

Another outfit with a proud history of producing young players is Freiburg, whose reserves won the German Under 19 FA Cup four times between 2006 and 2012, as well as three Under 19 championships over the same period.

During the 2012/13 campaign, Freiburg came close to doing the unimaginable and qualify for the Champions League – with a first team squad that contained ten home-grown players, and run on a wage budget of just €18million for players and staff. Brilliantly, part of the club ethos is that every senior academy player earns the same amount.

Led by manager Christian Streich – a former teacher who worked in the club's youth set-up for 16 years – they fell just short, finishing fifth after a final day shoot-out with Schalke, who pipped them with a dramatic 2-1 victory. Even in the biggest game in the club's history, Freiburg turned to youth, with teenager Sebastian Kerk handed a surprise debut. Four of their stars were promptly poached after that match – winger Daniel Caligiuri snared by Wolfsburg for €4.5million, Cedric Makiadi joining Werder Bremen for €3million, forward Max Kruse heading to Monchengladbach for €2.5million, and Johannes Flum signing for Frankfurt for €2million.

It's an increasingly common occurrence, with central defender Matthias Ginter the most recent prospect to be tempted away, joining Dortmund for €10million in 2014, as home-grown keeper Oliver Baumann joined Hoffenheim for €5.5million. The club's relegation in the 2014/15 season will make them even more vulnerable to such raids – but their constant supply of promising youngsters should make the club feel relaxed about their long-term future. As their famous Nineties chant goes: "We go down, we go up, we go into the UEFA Cup."

This supply has been developed over time. Freiburg were one of the earliest embracers of Germany's academy plan, building their €10million football school in 2001 following relegation from the Bundesliga. The school includes four pitches, and a mini stadium, as part of the facilities. They also work with five amateur feeder teams, who are sent a part-time coach to train eight- to 11-year-olds twice a week, with the most promising students invited to training camps during school holidays, and junior tournaments at weekends. The club invests €3.5million a year into its academy, around ten per cent of turnover.

There is a strong educational focus at Freiburg, with academy players encouraged to continue their studies around their football schedule, while a selection of the staff have backgrounds in teaching, so can help with homework. A group of 16 young players board at the club's academy building, through the DFB's nationwide elite schools programme.

This approach is taken with the youngsters' best interests at heart, with manager Streich explaining to *The Guardian* that their future outside of football is something Freiburg have to consider.

"When I went to Aston Villa eight years ago, I told them our players go to school for 34 hours a week. They said 'No, you're a liar, it's not possible, our players go for nine hours'.

"What do you do with the players who have for three years only had nine hours a week of school? They said: 'They have to try to be a professional or not'. We can't do that in Freiburg, it's wrong. Most players in our academy can't be professionals, they will have to look for a job. The school is the most important thing, then comes football.

"We give players the best chance to be a footballer, but we give them two educations here; if 80% can't go on to play in the professional team, we have to look out for them."

The community ethos of the club is another striking element – representing a town with a population of just 230,000 people, Freiburg is a tight-knit place. In the summer of 2013, after the club came so close to Champions League qualification, it was reported that all bar two of the club's 66 young players in the Under 16 to Under 19 age groups were eligible to play for Germany.

*

Another side to achieve surprise continental qualification was Augsburg, who finished the 2014/15 campaign in the heady heights of fifth position, earning a spot in the Europa League group stage in the process.

It completes yet another remarkable rise, with Augsburg having only gained top flight status for the first time in 2011. Five years earlier, they'd just returned to professional football.

Their stadium – which, as is the German way, has a sponsored name, and was built fairly recently, in 2009 – is quite unique in that more than a third of the space is for standing fans; the 30,660 capacity includes standing room for 11,034.

Of the twelve players to make more than 20 appearances during that incredible 2014/15 campaign, half had arrived on free transfers – while top scorer Raul Bobadilla had cost just £1.32million from Basel, and mainstay centre half Ragnar Klavan, who played more minutes than anyone else, was even less expensive at £220,000 from AZ Alkmaar.

Their approach certainly differs to most in the Bundesliga – with 16 different nationalities in their squad, which is made up of 'just' 49% Germans, though that is still a preferable ratio when compared to most Premier League clubs.

The recent successes are a dramatic improvement on the financial turmoil Augsburg went through in the mid-Nineties, which resulted in the DFB relegating them to the Bayernliga, the fourth tier. Club sponsor Informatec had vowed to provide security for the club's league place, but were unable to do so, and debts left Augsburg's future in doubt – with local entrepreneur Walther Seinsch stepping in to restructure the financial management, and help return them to professional status in 2002. Less than ten years later, they were in the big time.

And, despite their foreign legion, Augsburg are following the German academy route too – since 2008, their youth teams have achieved the following successes: Under 19 champions (2010, 2012), Under 19 runners up (2009), Under 17 champions (2015), Under 17 runners up (2008, 2010), Under 15 champions (2010). In 1993, they were the latest non-Bundesliga side to win a national youth championship, amid something of a golden age under the guidance of coach Heiner Schuhmann, including four cup titles in the same period, who was subsequently poached by Bayern Munich.

Chapter 10

*

As recently as 2008, Bundesliga side Paderborn were a provincial club – competing in the 3. Liga, the third tier of German football, having spent a season in the fifth tier in 2000/01. Fast forward a few years, and the club has been on a long-term plan of its own, emerging as a top-flight club, quite incredibly.

Vice President and Managing Director Martin Hornberger reflected fondly on the journey he has witnessed first-hand. He said: "Following the visionary leadership of our club's president Wilfried Finke, in 2004 we had two intentions: a new stadium and to be promoted to the second division.

"The target to be promoted was reached in 2005, when building started on the new stadium – but a long-lasting conflict with the neighbouring residents forced the club into a building freeze.

"In 2008, our stadium was finished, and we had one more year in the third division after relegation, but we managed to be promoted again in 2009. Then, in 2014, the club had its most important achievement, being promoted to the Bundesliga.

"In this exceptional season, the club was able to write off debts – of €4.7million – and furthermore establish even more professional conditions. Therefore, the club finally had the ability to start building a comprehensive training ground for the professionals and the whole youth department, including an administrative and functional building plus four pitches."

It's telling that the first thing Paderborn did with their newfound wealth – of sorts – following promotion was to reinvest into long-term gains, their youth and training set ups, and to clear their debt. In England, clubs coming up would be far more likely to splurge on big money signings and Premier League wages. In fact, though the club added ten new faces for their tilt at the top flight, each new addition cost an average of just £172,000.

But this has long been the way for Paderborn, who have had to be a bit more three-dimensional in their approach, as they've never had the platform to simply throw money at a problem.

Their priciest capture, at £616,000, midfielder Moritz Stoppelkamp was far from extravagant, scored the longest goal in Bundesliga history – a 90-yard volley from the edge of his own box – in September of Paderborn's first ever season in the top flight, as they reached the dizzying heights of top of the table, before faltering to relegation. But Paderborn are confident their youth programme will help them return.

Hornberger continued: "Developing youth training academies had a major impact on the whole German football structure. To focus on educating young talents is also one of the key aspects of the philosophy of Paderborn.

"Producing our own youth academy was important for the club. Previously, this was only a basic set up, primarily due to a lack of consistency – Paderborn's heritage is of many consolidations of other clubs until 1997 – and a low budget.

"The young players now are being trained under professional structures in a collaborative network including club school, association and representative teams. With our own residential school, we support young players as much as we can, providing them with remedial teaching and educational consultants.

"We are trying to give young players at regional level the best support we can and, therefore, one of our main intentions is to educate more young players to one day be able to be part of the first team.

"There are three subjects of education – besides the physical development, we are also working on the personality and the school matters. One of our key aspects, therefore, is a holistic education of talented children and teenagers. Our well-qualified employees in the youth academy are highly motivated, enthusiastic, and always targeting improvement. The structure and staying down to earth enables us to focus on a familiar atmosphere and closeness to officials."

The academy has already reaped success – most notably striker Nick Proschwitz, who Hornberger reveals generated €2.7millon when signing for Hull City during the 2012/13 season. Not that Paderborn are intent on becoming a selling club to survive – in fact, they are actively trying to 'establish a border' between their players and other clubs.

Hornberger explains: "We aspire for optimal individual promotion with maximum athletic success. Our coaches are working on mentality, the young players shall learn to handle success, but also with setbacks.

"They shall always identify with the club, pursue their goals in every aspect and generate self-confidence. These conditions shall represent unique features and establish a border between other clubs."

The interview comes just days after Paderborn's Under 23 team earned promotion to the Oberliga, the German fifth division – a cause for celebration at the club, but also renewed focus; their desire, now, is to have each junior team reach the highest division possible, while one of the DFB schools in the area is attempting to achieve Elite status.

*

FC Union Berlin are one of the most unique stories of German football, as one of the league's quirkiest outfits. Their ground, for instance, is called 'Stadium by the Old Forester's House' – given its forest setting – and has become famous for its annual Christmas Carol party and filling its pitch with 750 sofas for its World Cup Living Room event, where the fans could watch action from Brazil 2014.

It's quite a reimagining as, while some of the other clubs mentioned in this chapter have progressed from lower league sides to Bundesliga surprise packages, or fought financial difficulty, Union Berlin had to see off the Stasi.

In the Fifties, the club had a rivalry with Dynamo Berlin, run by Erich Mielke, the head of state security in East Germany, formed by an amalgamation of police teams in Dresden then moved into Berlin as the official Stasi team.

The supporters of Union Berlin, whose name hints at their allegiances, were equally forthcoming, chanting: "we want no Stasi swine" in clashes between the teams – and, since unification, they've had their wish, with Dynamo struggling in the lower leagues.

Union, though, have gone from relative strength to strength, firmly establishing themselves in the second tier – and flirting with promotion. The club's stadium has a capacity of 22,012, most of which is standing room, with space for nearly 18,000 people on the three sides of terracing. The other side, the club's swish new stand with 3,812 seats, was built at a time when the club were hard-up – so their supporters simply decided to build it themselves.

After raising the money for the extension and modernisation, more than 2,000 Union fans invested a reported 140,000 working hours to make it happen. With its rural setting and flash new stand, the stadium has been compared to a spaceship parked amongst the woods. It's the perfect demonstration of German fan power.

*

If that assortment of success stories isn't enough to have you brushing up on your GCSE German and pledging allegiance to the Bundesliga, then the summer of 2014 should have offered more than enough feel-good factor to tip you over the edge. At the Brazil World Cup, it all came good for Germany – all the diligent work and philosophising coming together in exquisite fashion, the global game uniting to hail the undisputed best in the world...

Chapter 11
Culmination, coronation, jubilation

Even as perennial favourites for every international tournament they enter – and with the third shortest odds to go the distance at Brazil 2014 – Germany went somewhat under the radar in the build-up to the tournament. Much, instead, focussed on the hosts – with the distinctive Neymar enjoying a great deal of attention – and of Argentina and Lionel Messi's bid to match up to the ghost of Maradona.

Reigning champions Spain, too, featured heavily in the pre-tournament chatter, whilst the understated nature of the Germany squad perhaps made them less of an attraction for the highlights packages put together by media companies the world over. Not that they were entirely written off, or cast as the dark horses – they were just the Germans, always there or thereabouts.

Germany had qualified for the finals with ease – dropping just two points as they topped a group including Sweden, whose 4-4 draw in Berlin was the only time the Germans hadn't taken maximum points. Others put up less of a fight, with Ireland thumped 6-1 in Dublin, and Kazakhstan dispatched 4-1 in Nuremberg. Mesut Özil took on a talismanic role, finishing as a surprise top-scorer with eight goals. Only Holland took as many points as Germany, 28, during qualification, as Joachim Löw's men cemented themselves as amongst the European favourites.

His squad, then, should have picked itself – but there was still room for a few surprises. The initial 30-man party included Under 21 captain Kevin Volland, the Hoffenheim star's first international call-up, while frontman Mario Gomez's injury struggles saw him excluded, even though many had thought he might be picked as something of a wildcard. That role, instead, went to veteran Miroslav Klose, who had scored just eight times in club football during the 2013/14 season for Lazio.

Chapter 11

Experienced keeper Rene Adler, once national first choice, failed to make the 30, with Ron-Robert Zieler preferred as third choice behind Manuel Neuer and Roman Weidenfeller.

Another uncapped starlet, Augsburg's Andre Hahn, was also a surprise inclusion, though neither he nor Volland would make the final 23 – but Dortmund's full back Erik Durm, Freiburg's centre back Matthias Ginter, and midfielder Christoph Kramer, all relative rookies with just five caps between them, would.

Surprise faces or not, Germany continued their qualification form and comfort – after warm-up draws against Poland (0-0) and Cameroon (2-2) in Germany, Löw and co. signed off with an emphatic 6-1 win over Armenia, Mario Götze scoring twice, before travelling to Brazil.

There, as chaos reigned all around them – Spain thumped 5-1 in their opening match by Holland (before losing out to Chile too) and England engaged in tense clashes with Italy and Uruguay, losing both narrowly – Germany gently eased through the gears, keeping their powder dry.

The biggest drama in the German camp during the early stages of the World Cup was the pre-tournament injury to Marco Reus, the Dortmund attacker struck down in the warm up friendly against Armenia with an ankle injury – a devastating blow given that he'd contributed five goals and three assists in six qualifiers. Shkodran Mustafi, an inexperienced defender, was called up in his place.

That shock would have helped the squad to focus, knowing how cruelly fate can intervene on an individual basis. They settled quickly, dispatching ten man Portugal with ease in their opening fixture, Thomas Muller grabbing a hat trick as they ran out 4-0 winners. If that started some hype around Germany, it was quickly dialled down after a surprise 2-2 draw with Ghana, before a narrow victory over Jürgen Klinsmann's United States, 1-0, secured qualification for the knockout stages.

At that point, it was all pretty much par for the course for Germany. Other sides garnered more excitement, including Belgium, whose 100% record underlined their pre-tournament dark horses tag. Meanwhile, four goals from Lionel Messi gave Argentina three wins from three and offered television executives the perfect excuse to

134

replay them endlessly. Colombia (inspired by James Rodriguez) and Louis Van Gaal's Holland also boasted a perfect record going into the knock out stages, while France and hosts Brazil were also in the mix, qualifying with seven points, like the Germans.

Each of those sides would progress to the last eight, but Germany were again going under the radar – needing extra time to see off Algeria 2-1. In fact, the African side dominated their more illustrious opponents in the first half, despite the odds being stacked against them pre-match.

The underwhelming display led the BBC's online match report to observe: "Löw's men will have to improve dramatically if they are to secure a first World Cup since 1990." Löw was forced to defend his under-fire squad, pointing to a relative injury 'crisis' as Mustafi was ruled out of the rest of the tournament, with Mats Hummels, Bastian Schweinsteiger, Jérôme Boateng, Lukas Podolski and Sami Khedira all struggling with knocks. Arsenal defender Per Mertesacker reacted angrily, pointing out quite fairly: "What do you want? Shall we play pretty and get kicked out in the semis again?"

It made for a lot of pressure on a tough quarter-final tie with France, who had beaten Nigeria 2-0 in the previous round, and seemed full of confidence. But a resolute Germany progressed with an entertaining 1-0 win – Hummels' first half header enough to secure victory, even if it wasn't pretty. In the German press afterwards, Löw was hardly hailed for guiding his men to a second World Cup semi-final during his reign – many commentators speculated over who might replace him, and others voiced their displeasure over three straight one-goal victories.

German journalist Alexander Osang wrote in *Der Spiegel*, one of Europe's best-read magazines: "It's as if Löw can no longer please anyone at all. When he played Philipp Lahm in midfield, people said he was being stubborn. When he moved him back into defence, as he did against France, people said he didn't have a spine. If he wins, it's because of the team; if he loses, it's his fault."

The pressure was mounting but, despite the negativity, results meant that they were in the final four of the World Cup for the fourth time in succession, without having really hit top gear; their opening round walloping of Holland seemingly an indication that they'd peaked too soon.

On the BBC's live coverage of the semi-final, host Gary Lineker asked his team of pundits who would win, as the two teams filed onto the pitch. Without hesitation, Alan Hansen – he of famously ill-fated predictions – bellowed 'Brazil, definitely', while Alan Shearer followed with 'Long night, [but] Brazil'. Only Rio Ferdinand disagreed.

What happened next, then, was totally unexpected – and would establish Germany as sudden and instant favourites. Their historic 7-1 win over Brazil was remarkable and, finally, the German side played with some freedom.

In one breathtaking six-minute spell, Die Mannschaft bagged four goals as they blew their hosts away ruthlessly. As Brazilian fans wept in the stands, the sides went in at half time with the score 5-0. There'd be no letting off after the break, either; Andre Schürrle grabbing two second half strikes, to inflict Brazil's joint worst defeat of all time.

The first goal came after just 11 minutes – Muller was inexplicably allowed to find space at the back post to volley home a Toni Kroos corner, notching his fifth goal of the tournament. Eleven minutes later, another defensive lapse allowed Germany to double their lead – Fernandinho's missed interception gifting Kroos possession on the edge of the box. His savvy throughball found Muller's angled run, and his lay-off was dispatched at the second time of asking by Miroslav Klose, making him the World Cup's all time record goalscorer.

Neither goal was vintage defending by the hosts, but each demonstrated a clinical edge in front of goal that Germany had struggled to find for much of the tournament.

From the subsequent kick off, Germany seized possession back immediately from their bewildered opponents, Özil fed Lahm down the right flank, and the captain's cross eventually found itself sitting up nicely for Kroos to smash home left-footed from twenty yards.

The quick-fire goals were dramatic and shocking – and the Brazil squad visibly crumbled on the pitch. To a man they were disconsolate, knowing that the game was over, less than half an hour in. As the German players returned to their half after celebrating, they would pick up on their opponents' dejection, and it would inspire confidence.

Again, straight from the kick off, as Brazil shakily tried to keep hold of the ball, Germany were at it – brimming with the belief that they'd already won the game – as Kroos robbed the hapless Fernandinho, before exchanging passes with Sami Khedira, and rolling the ball past a shell-shocked Julio Cesar.

Three minutes later, the fifth arrived, with centre back Hummels latching on to a wild clearance from David Luiz, and marauding forward freely. When the stand-in Brazil captain Luiz charged recklessly from his defensive line to try and rectify his error, Hummels was able to slide the ball into the space he'd left behind to Khedira, who played a one-two with Özil, before finding the net, in a repeat of the fourth goal. Barely 300 seconds after scoring their second, Germany were suddenly celebrating their fifth.

Schürrle added two after half time to take the tally to an incredible seven – first tapping home after good work from Lahm and Khedira on the right wing, before finishing with the best goal of the game, a rising effort on the half volley after taking the ball down in mid-air beautifully.

Incredibly, Brazil were able to rouse themselves for a late consolation – Oscar latching on to a long ball forward to beat Neuer with just seconds remaining on the clock. But his effort got more reaction from the German players than his own, furious that they'd squandered a clean sheet.

The official FIFA match report described the result as "the most extraordinary World Cup victory of all time", noting that Germany had become the first team in the tournament's history to score seven goals during a knockout phase fixture. And the British media grimly flagged that the Germans, in one game, had scored more goals than England had during their last two World Cup outings combined.

*

Chapter 11

Before the semi-final, headlines had centred on the uncertainty around Löw and how he needed to win the tournament to keep his job. After the match, it was almost a case of job done – though the worldwide coverage still preferred the obvious narrative around a certain diminutive forward they'd be facing in the final, as Argentina stood between Germany and a fourth World Cup success, in a repeat of the 1986 and 1990 deciders.

And, while Messi was awarded the Golden Ball, in contentious fashion, it was Germany that lifted the golden trophy that mattered – Götze's sublime extra time winner seeing off Argentina.

After a terse game of few chances – and those that did present themselves fell to the Argentines with first Gonzalo Higuain and then Messi spurning huge opportunities – the release around Götze's winner was understandable; most of the line-up surrounded the goalscorer, while the substitutes and coaching staff erupted on the bench.

Compared to the dominant performance against Brazil, Germany's showing in the final was an anxious affair, fraught with errors, perhaps best characterised by Kroos' – otherwise a star of the tournament – nervy back-pass that Higuain should have opened the scoring from. The Napoli frontman seized upon Kroos' uncharacteristic pass into no-man's land, a tentative header towards his keeper, but could only skew his finish horribly wide. Minutes later, he was celebrating wildly after finding the back of the net – only for Germany to be rescued by the offside flag. They were saved shortly afterwards by a goal-line clearance from Boateng, as Messi played the ball tantalisingly across the six yard box.

Those scares seemed to prompt Germany into some kind of life, having been as dazed as early casualty Christoph Kramer – who suffered a concussion in the opening stages – for much of the first half. That revival was led by Kramer's replacement, Schürrle, who demonstrated an urgency lacking elsewhere on the pitch – producing Germany's first real effort on goal, his vicious strike from distance well saved, particularly as Özil blocked the keeper's sight until the last moment. Then, with half time imminent, a Kroos corner was crashed against the post by Benedikt Höwedes.

But the second half began in the same way as the first, with Argentina on the front foot – and player of the tournament Messi was handed a golden opportunity to write his name above Diego Maradona's in Argentine folklore once and for all. A yard clear of the defence, having sprung the offside trap, the goal was at his mercy, the ball at his brilliant left foot – all he had to do was slide it past Neuer into the far corner. Somehow, he contrived to over-cook it, dragging his effort wide, letting Germany off the hook again.

With Messi subdued, and Argentina's huffing and puffing amounting to nothing, Germany grew into extra time – and Götze's goal felt inevitable, even if it was the first real opportunity they'd conjured for the best part of an hour.

As final matches go, it was nowhere near a classic, and though the result will define the squad, the performance certainly won't. It was arguably their poorest in Brazil.

*

In the aftermath, the plaudits and accolades flowed generously towards Löw and his men – with Rio Ferdinand saying during the BBC's live coverage: "This group of German players are going to be here for a long time and they are going to dominate."

If that seems a slightly hyperbolic and knee-jerk reaction, especially given that for various key players this was a final World Cup, Ferdinand was far from alone in this viewpoint – as, while Lahm, Schweinsteiger, Podolski and Mertesacker would most likely be moving on before 2018, along with the veteran Klose, Germany's glut of golden youngsters like Götze appear to have a glittering future ahead of them.

They possess a clutch of players who should be at, or approaching, their peak by the time Russia host international football's biggest event, including Özil, Hummels, Neuer, Höwedes, Khedira, Toni, Schürrle and Muller. While the boy wonder himself, Götze, could have another three World Cups in him.

Given that, and the pressure he'd overcome during the tournament, it's little wonder that Löw was in confident mood pre-match. He told the world's press: "We have young players who aren't even here and other players with a fantastic future such as Ilkay Gundogan, Marco Reus, Mesut Özil, André Schürrle and Thomas Muller.

"They can go on to play for a number of years. We can play on top of the world for a good number of years, with some young players coming in to reinforce the team. We know we can write history."

Upon their return home to Germany, for a victory parade in Berlin, the squad had emerged as the most sought-after in world football, with acclaim ringing in their ears – Neuer credited with being the best goalkeeper in the world, something his subsequent Balon d'Or nomination would testify to; Kroos completing a big money move to Real Madrid as he finished as joint-top assist provider during the tournament; Schweinsteiger hailed for his defensive nous having originally emerged as a winger, becoming Manchester United's top target the following summer; Lahm's versatility across several positions earning him rave reviews; and Muller lauded as the man who could do everything, after scoring five goals and setting up three more in Brazil.

At FIFA's 2014 Ballon d'Or ceremony – where Löw was named Best Coach – four of the top ten players in the Player of the Year vote were German, with Muller (5th), Lahm (6th) and Kroos (9th) following Neuer who came third. Neuer, Lahm and Kroos were all announced in the 2014 Team of the Year, too – though that title would surely have been better applied to Germany's World Cup winning squad.

Once considered definitive footballing foes, the German successes of 2014 illustrated a huge gulf between them and England, who were lacklustre in Brazil, displaying a World Cup outing that was typical of the preceding decade. But such underwhelming performances and consistent underachievement isn't a position entirely alien to Germany, who were themselves in a similar rut in the early 2000s. Given the way they've regenerated and re-emerged, there's much England can learn from their all-conquering rivals...

Chapter 12
Follow the Bundes-leaders: what the Premier League can learn

Fair ticket prices, on-field success, ever-expanding marketing revenue, an entertaining domestic league, and an all-conquering national team – it is little wonder that German football is the envy of the world game. But what lessons can be learned from the journey it has been on over the past 15 years?

As the only division in world football that can claim an edge on the Bundesliga – at least in terms of money and, erm, oft-claimed 'entertainment' – it might seem counter-intuitive for the Premier League to want to follow a league below them in the rankings. But, there's no doubt that the English game would do well to observe what's worked for Germany – and try to apply some of it.

While the Premier League wins plaudits and obscene television deals, match-going fans have become priced out and disillusioned with the game, while English players have been priced out of the first team – as queues of cheap foreign imports arrive at top-flight clubs in every transfer window, which in turn damages the national team. A split between the Premier League and the FA means that it's difficult for the two main bodies in English football to come together – and, when they do, the suggested solutions have been questionable. The idea of introducing Premier League reserve sides lower down the Football League pyramid, for example, to give young players competitive minutes and experience, was slammed by lower league clubs, and quickly revised.

Similarly, the tightening of home-grown quotas was seen as a smart decision, but criticism quickly emerged as Arsenal naturalised Cesc

Fabregas and, as soon as that loophole was closed, mega-rich sides like Manchester City simply stockpiled promising English players to tick a box rather than get them in the box. With playing time limited, the big names brought in from abroad were still first choice, and talent went wasted – the examples of Jack Rodwell and Scott Sinclair are often used to illustrate this point. While City's third-choice keeper Richard Wright has never played a competitive minute for the club, his initial one-year deal was extended several times simply because he was an easy way of taking up a home-grown spot. Having joined the Blues in 2012, he most recently signed a contract for the 2015/16 season, despite knowing that he is unlikely to even make the substitutes' bench during the campaign.

Both ideas, though, were rooted in some kind of logic – the B-team fiasco was ill conceived, but leant on what happens in Spain and, indeed, Germany, albeit in totally different footballing structures. The tradition of the Football League should be protected, but it does prevent the Premier League following the German model of competitive fixtures for reserve sides. The home-grown quota, too, works – but only if the young English players actually get onto the pitch.

With the Premier League wielding all the power in England, what exactly can the Football Association do to address the issue of the under-performing Three Lions on an international stage? In this case, it seems, following old rivals Germany isn't out of the question. Little more than ten years after the DFB scoured Europe for successful models to influence their reimagining, now others are coming to them for advice – including England. Dan Ashworth, who was appointed as Director of Elite Development by the FA in 2014, ensured German counterpart Robin Dutt was one of his first visits, spending three hours with the former Freiburg coach to pick his brain.

One of the messages Dutt passed on might well have been that the FA need to be more proactive – the DFB's development programme often spots players before they are affiliated with a club, making their weekly training session a must-attend for many Bundesliga scouts. In England, the FA relies on clubs to spot and nurture talent, but the DFB are happy to do some of the youth recruitment for their clubs. As Dutt told *The Guardian*: "If we help the clubs, we help us, because the players of our national teams – the youth teams and Joachim Löw's team – come from the clubs.

"It would be better for England if the clubs and the association talked together. If you see the English clubs, there are a lot of foreign players and not many from England. Chelsea win the Champions League and then the Europa League, so they have success. But the English national team, I don't think they are successful at this time."

In Germany, the academy focus has been fundamental in everything good that has come over the past decade and a half – proving the starting point itself for the DFB's 10-year plan. Now, everyone in the German set up is a convert. Although, it seems, the academy has long been a priority for clubs – if Michael Ballack's memories of his career starting point are anything to go by.

He said: "To pay attention to your academies is always good. I grew up in East Germany, and we had this school called Teach and Youth Sport Schools, where you could actually train and do your schoolwork together, organised perfectly.

"Football was a really big subject, so you would train more than other kids. In the time when the other kids had sport, you would do your football training. So you have your advanced training, but still do your school work.

"The amount of training we did was better, and the standard was too, because the coaches actually worked for the school. And that's the system that worked really well in East Germany, and was developed across Germany over the 10-year plans.

"Kids get motivated, you bring them in school and you also have this subject orientated sports school where they can enforce the training without actually losing the view for the school.

"The best thing you can do is give attention to the academies and the kids, because they will pay it back in the long term for sure."

Certainly, there are plenty of horror stories from the English academy system, with young players finding their progress stunted – caught in the no man's land between the irrelevance of reserve league football, and the huge step up to competitive first team action. The classic example, here, is Josh McEachran at Chelsea – who made his first team debut at the age of 17, becoming the first player born after the Champions League started to take part in the competition, as he was named the club's Young Player of the Year. From January 2012 to the summer of 2015, though, the midfielder didn't make a single Chelsea appearance, going out on five different loan spells in the pursuit of regular football, before leaving to join Brentford permanently, his career in danger of stalling completely.

Someone who's had similar frustrations in an English side's youth team is promising forward Osayamen Osawe, who came through the ranks at Blackburn Rovers, where he struggled to get a look in, and ended up moving abroad in search of game-time – landing in Germany, with third-tier Hallescher FC.

"I signed for Blackburn when I was 12, and stayed there till I was 18. One of the age groups above me had five players break through into the first team – the likes of Phil Jones and Grant Hanley – while Blackburn were in the Premier League. So it seemed like a good time for youth, but after those players, it just seized up - and youth wasn't really given a chance. Only one player from my age range broke through. [John O'Sullivan who, at the time of writing, has only made three first team appearances for Rovers.]

"I spent a season on loan at Southport, in the fifth division, and that's when I realised I needed to move on. I came to Germany for a fresh start because it felt like I was never going to break through at Blackburn.

"England should definitely look at how Germany approaches youth. Bundesliga clubs have second teams in the game, which is great for young players as it gives you valuable experience.

"I played two or three years of Under-21 football, and that just doesn't prepare you for the men's game - it's a huge step up. That's something I found out from going out on loan, and is why so many young British players struggle after they've been stuck in reserve football.

"Giving young players competitive experience like that of men's football is the reason the German national team is doing so well, they're getting a good level of football. When I first came, I found it quite different to football in England, especially in training. For example, here, they have a trainer and a manager - in England, they're the same person, here it's two people.

"In terms of style of football, in England we press from the front usually, but I've found here that we drop to the halfway line and then press. So it took a while to adjust. But I've come to Germany to play, because I wasn't getting an opportunity in England. This season (2014/15), I've played more than twenty first team games."

It's becoming more common for English talent to head to Germany. Chelsea defender Michael Mancienne joined Hamburg in 2011 after just four league appearances for the Blues in five years. 49 Bundesliga games later, he returned to England with Nottingham Forest as an established first team player. England youth international Mandela Egbo, who was part of the squad that won the European Under 17 championships in 2014, joined Borussia Monchengladbach at the end of the following season, joining up with their Under 23 side rather than staying in Crystal Palace's reserves.

Osayamen's criticisms of the English game are well versed, and even those running the game would probably sympathise. The forward's call for more competitive youth football reflects the FA's plan for a 'League 3', where Premier League B teams would take on lower league clubs. Though that proved controversial, given the tradition of the English leagues, former German defender Jens Nowotny believes that a move in this direction is key to youth development – even if it means antagonising the Football League.

Reviewing English struggles, he said: "The biggest problem for the English game is that they don't do anything for the youth. The youth teams play but the occasion isn't good, because it doesn't matter.

"They only want to advertise the Premier League – it's that league for everybody, to take money. Anything else behind it doesn't matter, it isn't interesting for the clubs or fans. The clubs like to buy huge players from other countries more than they like to educate their own players. That's the problem.

"In Germany, they put money into youth education, and this is the right way. A 10-year plan is a good one for the Premier League – but you have to change now, not in ten years. The greatest problem is to plan for ten years then nothing happens."

Certainly, those involved at the top level of German football agree with Nowotny – there needs to be a way to make youth football competitive in England. There, kids as young as 11 are training regularly at a specific football school – which isn't dissimilar to the frequency that English youngsters train – but with competitive league matches at the end of the week to work towards. Their divisions offer titles and relegation, an incentive for putting the work in. Such an experience in England wouldn't happen until the Under 18 level.

Dutt, who replaced Matthias Sammer as Sporting Director of the German FA in 2012, before returning to club management with Werder Bremen a year later, said of this attitude: "It's important for the mentality to have some games in the year you have to win, but it is not the main thing. The main thing is to do good training. For the Germans this system is very important. It's like golf. If I play golf in England, no club wants to know my handicap. If I go to play in Germany you have to show your handicap. If you play with a guy you don't know, the first question is: 'How do you do?' The second question is: 'What is your handicap?' Germans want to reach something, they want to go up."

And Frank Arnesen, who has worked in both England and Germany – as Sporting Director at Chelsea, Tottenham and Hamburg – reasserts the belief that first team football is the be all and end all for promising youngsters.

In an interview with *The Guardian*, the Danish legend opined: "The money is a big part of the problem in England because clubs go out and buy finished players instead of waiting. Young players need to make mistakes to get better, but managers think they can't afford [for] that to happen. You see the squads, even in the smaller clubs, they get players from all over instead of bringing young players through.

"I think one thing is very important, coaches who are coaching for the national team of Germany, from upstairs to down, they are very respected and it's a good job to have. In England, I am not so sure about that. I think there is a feeling that to work for a club is much higher than [working for] the FA but that's not the case in Germany. The FA [must] create a situation where it is an honour to be there and you need help from clubs."

The experts don't lie – and nor do the numbers. It comes as little surprise, given their success domestically and internationally, that Germany offer the most opportunities to younger players – with the lowest average age of all the big leagues in Europe – while the number of foreign players in the Bundesliga is lower than each of their rivals bar La Liga. The second tier in Germany, meanwhile, outdoes the top division in both categories. That's based on figures taken from *Transfermarkt.co.uk* for the 2014/15 season.

Division	Number of players	Foreign players	Average age (years)
Bundesliga	505	241 (47.7%)	25.4
Premier League	557	361 (64.8%)	26.8
La Liga	467	191 (40.9%)	26.7
Serie A	552	300 (54.4%)	27.2
Ligue 1	530	254 (47.9%)	25.6
2. Bundesliga	507	160 (31.6%)	25.1
English Championship	735	389 (52.9%)	25.4

And, perhaps more strikingly, the proportion of foreigners in the Premier League is the highest by a considerable distance – almost 20% more than in the Bundesliga, and close to a quarter above the mark for home-grown friendly Spain. While the average Premier League player is older than all of their 'big five' equivalents, with the exception of the notoriously greying Serie A. A similar comparison between the two countries' second tiers shows a similar disparity in home-grown players.

These are issues that the FA is well aware of, leading to the opening of St George's Park – the National Football Centre – in 2012. In the same way that the Germans looked upon France's Clairefontaine for inspiration, the 330-acre site in Burton-upon-Trent was bought in 2001, around the same time as the German crisis talks, for £2million. Actual building work was delayed until 2008.

It takes in 12 training pitches, a full-size indoor pitch, a replica of the Wembley pitch, an altitude chamber, state of the art hydrotherapy pools, biomechanics and training gyms, video analysis suites, and sport science facilities. On site, a Hilton Hotel provides accommodation for the teams that are in residence. As well as the various England squads that meet and train there, St George's Park has also hosted various teams from across Europe – including Monaco, Galatasaray, and Steaua Bucharest.

In the coaches' room is a huge clock, mounted on the wall, counting down. The final date is set for the start of the 2022 World Cup in Qatar. Its purpose is to challenge England to become world champions before that countdown reaches zero, a long-term target that has been set as a motivational tool. Whether that's quite long-term enough, though, is another matter entirely.

But, there are green shoots of promise, if only a handful. The Under 21s finished second to Germany at the 2009 European Championships. At the Under 19 level, they are the most successful ever nation – winning the competition nine times alongside Spain – though they haven't qualified for the finals since 2012, when they reached the semi-finals.

The Under 17s reached the quarter-finals in 2015, having won the competition in 2014, when they were led by the likes of Chelsea forward Dominic Solanke, Newcastle striker Adam Armstrong, and Fulham playmaker Patrick Roberts, who was poached by Manchester City in July 2015.

It's younger age groups like this that lead Matt Crocker, the FA's head of player development, to boldly state in an interview with *The Times*: "I truly believe our [young] players are as good as anyone's – I've seen it. Without a doubt, we should be challenging in 2022 — and beyond that because it's not just a one-off target. The talent is, genuinely, on a par with anywhere in the world. There are things we can't control in terms of their development, but there's an awful lot we can. There are no excuses."

But if anyone recognises talent when they see it, Crocker is as good a judge as any – having overseen the progression of Gareth Bale, Luke Shaw, Theo Walcott and Alex Oxlade-Chamberlain, amongst a slew of prodigies, while managing the Southampton academy.

The current breed of young talent is getting those in the England setup almost as excited as they were over the last batch of Three Lions stars that emerged together – though the Golden Generation never quite lived up to its billing. And there are concerns now that the likes of Solanke and Roberts won't even get to recreate the club success that group enjoyed – as they struggle to get a look-in at domestic level.

At Chelsea, in particular, there is a batch of youngsters who are considered amongst the best in the world – reaching four straight FA Youth Cup finals between 2012 and 2015, winning three, taking their tally to four titles from six, and six finals from eight. In 2014, the Blues were the Under 21 Premier League champions and, in 2015, they won the UEFA Youth League in its second season of existence.

Solanke, 18 in September 2015, and who notched up 41 goals at youth level, was invited to train with the full England squad during the 2014/15 campaign. He did so alongside midfielder Ruben Loftus-Cheek, who made his first-team debut towards the end of the same season; winger Izzy Brown, who did likewise; and Lewis Baker, who meanwhile spent loan spells with Sheffield Wednesday and MK Dons. All are expected to break through. Their success appears to have motivated Jose Mourinho to offer younger charges a chance in the first team.

He said, during the pre-season tour of summer 2014: "My conscience tells me that if, for example, Baker, Brown and Solanke are not national team players in a few years, I should blame myself. They are part of a process the club started without me. In this moment, we have players who will be Chelsea players – and when they become Chelsea players, they will become England players, almost for sure."

This generation of player have even higher expectations internationally than in club football. With previous eras criticised for a perceived lack of pride, the FA launched an 'England DNA' project in December 2014, aimed at the likes of Solanke and Brown. It intends to define an identity and style of play for future England players.

Part of the FA's manifesto, launched by Crocker, director of elite development Dan Ashworth and Under 21 head coach Gareth Southgate, reads: "The backstories of players in the England setup are wide and varied with many players of multicultural background in our teams. The diversity of our England players is to be celebrated.

"England teams aim to intelligently dominate possession selecting the right moments to progress the play and penetrate the opposition."

Chapter 12

Speaking of the production of the blueprint – which, in many ways, seems to be the equivalent of Germany's 10-year plan – Ashworth said: "When I first arrived at the FA 18 months ago, we looked at international success. We looked at seven European countries, ourselves includes, and three South American countries – the ones who had been most successful in getting to tournaments.

"We looked at the differences between those teams and the nations who went on to win things. The successful teams tended to have players who had more experience at international level, more caps. One of the reasons was because our competitors had more teams than us, so we have introduced an Under 15s, Under 18s and Under 20s to keep those teams and players connected."

However, the failure of the England Under 21s side at the 2015 European Championships – the third successive tournament at which the team was knocked out in the first round stage – prompted an avalanche of criticism, and mockery when Ashworth, Southgate and the like repeated the claim that the senior team could still win the 2022 World Cup.

Most of the ire, though, was reserved for the 'big time charlie' stars who didn't join up with the squad for the tournament – senior internationals Raheem Sterling, Ross Barkley, Jack Wilshere and Phil Jones were all eligible for selection, but not taken on the grounds that they were established full internationals. As Dan Ashworth insisted: "It's like being a first-team player and asking them to come back and play in the Under 21s. It's not necessarily the right thing to do."

But others were less forgiving, notably Joey Barton, who blasted young England stars on *Radio 5 Live*: "As some players get towards the top, they say: 'I'm too good for the Under 21s because I've been in an England senior squad and I don't want to go to a tournament because I need to rest.'

"They're not available because they're saying 'it would be better for my career not to go to this tournament', or their managers at club level are saying 'we're not going to do that'.

"The FA should just say to them 'look, if you don't make yourselves eligible for an Under 21 campaign if you're selected, then you won't be considered for the national side for however many years'."

Certainly, the same value isn't put on coming through the ranks in England as it is in Germany. Instead, the Premier League's latest flavour of the month is usually fast-tracked into the senior team, with the Under 21 side struggling to attain much credibility, even as a stepping-stone into international action. To illustrate the point, even Tom Ince, who had spent the previous season out of favour at Hull City, as the Tigers failed to beat relegation, decided to rule himself out of Under-21 contention in March 2015.

Danny Mills, a former international who was part of an FA commission set up to assess potential improvements to the national game, spoke of the gap between England and Germany while explaining the struggles of the Under 21 side, who he said were given too much too young.

He told the *BBC*: "[Players are] given so much so early in club football that England Under 21s has become secondary. There isn't the same desire to play for them. Spain and Germany still have the desire to play for their Under 21s – they get paid an awful lot less than our players.

"English players are paid too much and clubs put pressure on them not to go to the tournament. We have to change this culture. Things don't change overnight – changing the way England play and players develop will take ten years at least. That's what the Germans had to do before becoming very successful."

While the FA and associates point the finger at the Premier League's culture – and quite rightly, too – that's not to say they get everything right when it comes to appealing to their players. Indeed, former captain Steven Gerrard highlighted an oversight in the planning of St George's Park – something for the players to do in their downtime.

He told *BT Sport*: "It's an unbelievable site but they need to be a bit more realistic around it. They need to make it a little friendlier for the players. It's a top place to train and prepare but, away from the training pitch and the games, it can be boring. We need to create that atmosphere where England players are desperate to get away and do well.

"When you get to England, you want to have your lunch and go to bed and keep away from everyone because there's a shyness. There needs to be an England atmosphere when you turn up and you know each other – you want to be with each other."

It's a flashback to one of the exact changes that Jürgen Klinsmann made upon his appointment as Germany manager in 2004. More than a decade on, and England are still behind the times – although they might finally be catching up as, within hours of Gerrard's criticism, plans for a nine-hole golf course were announced at St George's.

And even the Premier League have acknowledged a duty to address the dearth of home-grown stars emerging within their clubs' youth systems – although it should also be pointed out that this will help protect their brand, too – following the implementation of the Elite Player Performance Plan, better known as EPPP, in 2012.

Controversially, particularly from the perspective of Football League minnows, the EPPP freed up the movement of young players by abolishing the previous 90-minute rule for catchment areas – meaning giants like Manchester United and Chelsea could snap up youngsters from a wider geography, at a fixed fee, from other academies.

A key principle of the plan, which should be lauded, is to ensure more playing and training time for home-grown talent, and to broker relationships between clubs and local schools – something that is already the norm in Germany.

The demands on clubs signing up to the EPPP, though, are intense, and certainly Premier League scaled; Category 1 academies require a minimum of 18 full-time staff and an operational budget of £2.5million. While the rewards of investing in such a way and unearthing a gem have been limited, with independent tribunals scrapped in favour of set prices, Liverpool signing a 15-year-old Raheem Sterling from QPR today would cost them between £12,500 and £40,000 initially, plus a maximum of £1.3million in appearance fees if he had gone on to play 100 top-flight games for the club. That falls well short of the £5million deal brokered in 2010 when he was 'poached' from the Rangers academy. And they'd almost certainly not be entitled to the 25% of Sterling's subsequent sale to Manchester City for £49million, which banked them close to £10million.

With players available from as little as £3,000 under the new EPPP rules, it's really not much of a surprise that various clubs – including Wycombe Wanderers and Yeovil Town – folded their academies in reaction to its introduction. The first initial of the programme, Elite, is seemingly the most appropriate.

*

But it's not just player development where England lags behind Germany. The depth in coaching resources, too, shows a staggering gulf. According to UEFA figures from 2013, Germany had 28,400 coaches with their B license – compared to a paltry 1,759 in England. The gap continued at A license level, 5,500 vs 895, and was most worrying at the top level, the Pro license, which is the highest qualification available, as Germany boasted almost ten times as many coaches – 1,070 compared to England's 115.

The inclusion of a coaching rethink, then, was not a shock when the England DNA project was unveiled in late 2014, with the governing body issuing directives for a training philosophy – including demands that every session has at least "70% rolling ball time", and is reviewed afterwards.

However, documents filled with management mumbo-jumbo aside, England needs to be doing more to encourage coaches to train and qualify – by showing them opportunities and incentives exist if they do. This is according to Christian Streich, the Freiburg manager who rose through the ranks from Under 19 coach to main man, a route rarely trodden in English football.

He told *The Guardian*: "They have to look to build coaches in England. They have a lot of money and they have bought players. But for me the most important thing is to educate the coaches in the youth academies. Before in Germany, if you played in the Bundesliga for a few years, clubs said: 'We'll take them to manage the under-17s.' But they had no education to be a coach. Sometimes the same thing happens in England. On the pitch these players played very well but that doesn't mean they're a coach, and now this changes in Germany. And then under-15, under-17 and under-19 coaches, they gave them a salary so they could do this work full time. Coaches came from university, who had studied sport, they mixed it up and then it got better."

This is an area where England, and in particular the FA, are making a concerted effort to catch up – but the sheer volume difference in terms of their coaching pool when compared to Germany is astounding, and says much about the current disparity between the two national teams.

*

Another eye-opening area of contrast between the Premier League and the Bundesliga – the two divisions vying for global acclaim – is in ticket prices. Ah yes, the fans that *aren't* watching on TV. In England, these spectators, generally, are taken as a given in the top-flight – someone who, no matter what, will always want to take that seat. For the Premier League bigwigs, there's definitely been a greater prioritisation towards viewers from far away – Asia, Africa, South America, and so on – when compared to the regulars in their stands.

Critics will argue that English football boards have been too busy tap-dancing to the tune of lucrative revenue streams in the Far East and other far flung places – shipping players to Dubai, say, for an inconvenient end of season friendly, while tours of the States are commonplace pre-season, even if managers such as Louis Van Gaal don't think they help his squad's preparation. Meanwhile, those closer to home have been overlooked and, for some, even exploited – with ticket prices soaring for the local fans that generate the famous Premier League atmosphere.

As we've explored earlier – in *Chapter Six* – the Bundesliga is the antithesis of this, running a truly fan-friendly operation. And that hasn't gone unnoticed. Ask anyone what the Premier League could learn from its German counterpart, and the phrase 'ticket prices' is sure to form part of their opening gambit.

It's a philosophy that is embraced by everyone involved in the German game – as World Cup winning midfielder Christoph Kramer explained: "The atmosphere at Bundesliga games has clearly improved in recent years. Especially when you see the English ticket prices, of course you have to say that in Germany the prices are low, and I think that's important because everyone should have the chance to see a game. That's why the stadiums are always full, and have great atmospheres."

Kramer was complimentary about English football, though, observing that, despite its disregard for their fans' pockets, it still boasts the best product – for now. "I think that the Premier League is still actually the best league in the world, because there are quite a lot of top stars there, and the play is up and down – it is a very intense game there. The ball is always played forward, there is a lot of power in it, and that's nice and easy to see watch. There is no messing around at the back, before long the audience would whistle, but the ball is always cut to the front and then they go, which is obviously attractive for the spectators to watch."

Someone who was less generous in his comparison, though, is former Celtic, Aston Villa and Bayern Munich forward Alan McInally. To him, it's quite clear that the Premier League has much to learn from the Bundesliga – and the process should have started long ago.

He said: "The English FA should follow the way the Germans do things. They should've done it when Germany did it, in 2004, after that really bad tournament. It's a good thing that our FA have said they'd like to follow their lead, because the price of tickets in Germany is better.

"Obviously, you can still get expensive tickets with a nice bite to eat if you want it, but the Bundesliga has an availability of tickets for £15 to £30 to go and see a football match. You'd struggle in England to do that, even in the Championship.

"The model is pretty good in Germany, and I'm not surprised the FA are looking at it – they're doing it right, and it's not affecting the clubs in a way where they're not being competitive in Europe.

"I'd like to hope we have the patience to go with a ten year plan in Britain, but we might need to change our attitude a little bit. That would have to come from the FA, and then be agreed to by the majority of the clubs from the top right down to the bottom of the Football League.

Chapter 12

"The Premier League is the most sought-after league to be watched and played in, that monster might stop the sort of patience needed for England to develop.

"But if you look at German football at the moment, they absolutely obviously got it right. So that's the incentive. And, if the top eight of the Premier League want to adhere to the Financial Fair Play rules that have come in from UEFA, they've got to invest in their youth set-up anyway."

A major stumbling block, McInally warns, is that the Premier League is juggling a phenomenon unknown to the Bundesliga – a breed of super-rich young players, who can be millionaires several times over without ever having to establish themselves as first team players. In 2011, Liverpool spent £2million on an unknown 14-year-old, Oluwaseyi Ojo, to sign him from MK Dons, for instance. He's still yet to play for them, though, at 18 he has plenty of time.

Young players of that ilk – admittedly through no fault of their own – are suddenly parachuted into a culture of excess, and materialistic expectations, as Frank Lampard put it, in an interview with *The Times*: "Clubs are desperate to sign the best young talent, so money is thrown at them, they get a bit of fame, and it's human nature that some take their eye off the ball. Money creates an atmosphere where very young kids think they've made it. As soon as one [player] comes in a Range Rover, it's natural for the other kids to think 'I need one of those'."

Wilfried Zaha, a £15million signing for Manchester United in January 2013, aged just 21, was reported to have splurged out on four cars in the five months following the transfer – before he'd even joined up with the United squad, having been immediately loaned back to Crystal Palace. Eventually, he didn't make the cut at Old Trafford, and returned to South London two years later. Presumably in a very nice car.

For McInally, this is symptomatic of the ills burdening English football. He lamented: "British kids want everything immediately, they want success tomorrow, rather than having to wait to get your opportunity in the first team – and do you really need to get in the first team because you're already on big money before you get there.

"I'd like to see a bigger carrot dangled in front of British youngsters for success, rather than 'I've signed my first professional contract, I'm going to be a millionaire before I'm 19'. I don't see the point of that, unless they're exceptional.

"If they're playing in the reserve or youth team, and want silly money, let them go, see if someone else is stupid enough to give them it – and you know where it'll be, it'll be at one of the bigger clubs, where they might never play football."

The irony is, these wealthy young men who can buy supercars and designer labels as teenagers, are unlikely to be cheered on by their non-footballer mates – as teen football fans are priced out of the Premier League, and much of English football.

From a German fan's perspective, ticket pricing is one of the two biggest attractions – the other being the buoyant Bundesliga atmospheres, especially when compared to the relatively stale ambience of many Premier League grounds. It is a consequence of the conscious decision to keep costs down for supporters.

And it has attracted more than 1,000 English fans, who travel to Germany to watch Dortmund every week. One such British-based BVB fan, George Docherty, from Edinburgh, explained how sensible pricing is badly needed in the UK – in tandem with standing at football, which is probably number three on the Bundesliga list of plus points: "Britain could learn a lot from the pricing, or from having at least one side of the stadium standing. What they forget over here is that football fans can be their own best police, we don't need stewards to tell us where to go. Keep an eye on fans, but don't treat them like children.

"In Scotland, you're queuing up for a game, and you're treated like kids going into assembly. We know how to queue and go through a turnstile. At the end of the day, we're paying customers, and I don't know any other business that would treat their customers like football fans are in Britain.

"As soon as you put on football colours here, immediately you're a target – but it's a source of pride in Germany. Outside Dortmund, before the game, it's a sea of yellow and black, all waving massive flags – try taking one of those into a game over here, they're seen as a potential murder weapon."

Chapter 12

Unsurprisingly, German fans are proud that the game there welcomes them – and deeply oppose the English style of governance. In February 2015, following the Premier League's announcement of a record TV rights deal worth more than £5billion, Bayern Munich fans reacted by holding up a banner reading 'This ain't no Premier League', making their opinion of the English game very clear.

*

Despite everything, there's probably a sense of 'what if' amongst FA bigwigs. They might not admit it publicly, but there must be a nagging thought that Germany's humiliation of England at the 2010 World Cup might never have happened should Frank Lampard's now infamous 'ghost goal' been allowed to stand. At that stage, it would have made the game 2-2 at half time, and Germany may not have been able to run away with it.

England might even have dragged proceedings out to penalties, before departing the tournament with some credit in the bank – rather than seeing Mesut Özil inspire a rampant second half display against a side that appeared to give up. Be that as it may, the result should have acted as a wakeup call for England. Certainly, supporter expectations crashed down to earth – and a rather meek Euro 2012 showing, where they were beaten on penalties by Italy in the quarter-final, earned relatively positive reviews with the German mauling in mind.

Further disappointment in the 2014 World Cup served as a reminder of the work that needs to be done. Speaking in the aftermath, England coach Gary Neville admitted that the Germans were a step ahead – but was unsure they could be followed, tweeting: "We are going to have to find our way of doing it because the system we have doesn't allow us to adopt the German route in its entirety. I'm confident the mountain is starting to move, but it's a slow shift and results will take time."

Arsenal midfielder Jack Wilshere, seen as a pivotal part of the current regeneration of the England team – manager Roy Hodgson has even created a role specifically for him in front of the defence – has also acknowledged that Germany offers a role model to follow, especially as the Golden Generation have been put out to pasture, and a new era of players emerges.

He told *The Telegraph*: "It's been a big ask for the young players, [Jordan] Henderson and myself. When we lost players like Steven Gerrard and Frank Lampard, who have been a big part of the national team for ten years, there was a bit of pressure. We have come a long way from then, and we feel we have a long way to go before the Euros [2016].

"We feel we can give it a go. Remember when Germany lost all their big players and they started again with Özil, [Sami] Khedira and the others, when they were in South Africa? They had a really good World Cup and they were a bit unlucky if we're honest. Now look at them. That's the way we want to go."

Even Germans are telling England to follow their model – their most-capped player of all time, Lothar Matthäus wrote a brilliant piece for the *Daily Mail* on the eve of the 2014 World Cup, spelling out exactly why the FA need to look to Germany's re-emergence.

Brutally, and pulling no punches, he wrote: "If England want to continue coming home from major tournaments after two weeks, and watching the final on TV, there is a simple enough way – keep ignoring top young talent like Ross Barkley and Luke Shaw.

"I'm willing to bet there are a lot of potential Rooneys in England... longing for someone to show belief in them. Mark my words, England will reap the benefits [if they do put faith in youngsters] – possibly immediately, certainly in the long term. These lads will only get better with experience. If anyone remains unsure, they should cast their minds back to what happened in Germany at the turn of the century."

These benefits have been acknowledged by Roy Hodgson – who has revealed he was once close to becoming manager of Germany in 1998, and has displayed more of a long-term attitude than his predecessors, having his office at St George's Park – openly admitting that he had looked to Germany for inspiration.

He said: "I think the German FA were very wise in their attitude to changing the face of the national team and building it on youth and a very energetic style of play. Of course, as a result, the success they've had has not surprised anybody because we all know how good the players are… how strong the league is.

"The German team has become something of an example for many other European teams who might find themselves in a transitional period that Germany obviously found themselves in going into the 2006 World Cup. As far as we are concerned, we are perhaps to some extent in that transitional period."

The incentive for him and the FA to follow the German blueprint is clear for all to see. Having been amongst the top three ranked sides in the world between 1993 and 1998, Germany disappeared somewhat from football's top table, before returning to the top three of FIFA's rankings in 2010, as their young side started to come good. In 2014, they topped the list for the first time since 1993. England, by comparison, peaked at third position in 2012 – itself a dubious over-rating.

And the Premier League, often so at odds with the Football Association, also have motivation to get on board with a German-esque plan. In 2012, the Bundesliga reaped the benefits of their factory-style academy system, as seven teams from the league entered European competition, all reaching the knockout stages for the first time.

But we have a way to go before accepting German approaches fully – Felix Magath, the only German to manage in the Premier League, was widely mocked when it was revealed that he had ordered defender Brede Hangeland to treat a knee injury with cheese. That, though, only tells half the story – Magath had simply suggested trying an old wives' tale, as little else seemed to be working.

Amid the media frenzy when this anecdote emerged, Magath retorted: "I'm as convinced as ever that English football has something to learn from German qualities. Unfortunately, they're reluctant to accept things."

Certainly, one of the things English fans and players alike would struggle to get their head around is the German use of homeopathic medicine – a controversial and divisive medical approach which believers claim can encourage the body to heal itself. In the top two leagues of German football, the practice is rife – with 92% of clubs treating players with homeopathic remedies. It's something you'd struggle to imagine someone like Harry Redknapp embracing.

*

For an England fan, the past chapter may well have been as difficult to read as it was to watch our various defeats to Germany – who, clearly, are better than us at our own game at the moment. But not everything is entirely rosy in the German garden – in fact, there are some downsides that they will be keen to weed out if their dominance is to continue...

Chapter 13
The downsides

So, having waxed lyrical about the German game over the past 50,000 words, raving about their success domestically and in the international arena, is the Bundesliga really the perfect league – and are Germany dead certs to repeat the World Cup success of 2014 in the coming years?

The answer to both questions, of course, is no – obviously not. Though the negatives are far out-weighed by the positives – this chapter is testament to that, a single section amid an entire book of praise – there are still some flaws in the German game, something the DFB and DFL would readily admit; there are few as hypercritical as their players and clubs, determined not to get carried away with their own success.

The biggest and most obvious criticism to levy at the Bundesliga revolves around their dominant force, Bayern Munich, who are so far above their competition that they make the division the closest thing to a one-horse race amid Europe's Big Five. Certainly, when held up against the Premier League – so often a favourable comparison throughout this book – it doesn't look great for the league; there are three or four English clubs that can realistically consider themselves title challengers each season, and that is a huge factor in the Premier League's global appeal, something Germany is trying to replicate.

One of the bigger worries for DFB chiefs, then, must be how to cultivate a more competitive league. They will, quite rightly, point to Dortmund's back-to-back successes in 2011 and 2012, plus their Champions League final face-off with Bayern in 2013, but the truth is that such periods are brief interruptions rather than a long-term changing of the guard, as evidenced by the gradual slide of BVB since that Wembley final.

German poster-boy Thomas Muller, a remarkably versatile star, the like of which England could only dream of, perhaps surmised it best, when (as touched upon in *Chapter 9*) he remarked that Bayern Munich training was more competitive than some league games: "It is often more difficult to win against our training team than maybe against a team in the Bundesliga." He might have said it with more than an air of mischief, but it rung true. Bayern's reserves would be first-team regulars elsewhere – highly rated Swiss winger Xherdan Shaqiri couldn't get much of a look-in during his three-year stint at the club, so was offloaded to Inter Milan, hardly a small-time outfit.

And this gulf in class has told in continental clashes since Bayern lifted the Champions League in 2013. The lack of challenge in domestic ties – they thumped Hamburg 8-0 in 2015, and between 2013 and 2015 beat Werder Bremen 7-0, 5-2, 6-0 and 5-0 – saw Bayern heavily beaten by Real Madrid and Barcelona in successive seasons, losing 5-0 on aggregate to Madrid in 2014, and 5-3 to Barcelona a year later. When you are preparing for super-clashes, you don't want to have been simply going through the motions in second gear for the past few weeks; such build-ups left Bayern susceptible to fellow European giants, who exploited this softness with glee.

Seeing as Germany have effectively placed all of their eggs in one basket, with Bayern representing them in Europe, it is a worrying development that the league will be well aware of – everyone benefits from a more competitive division. Bayern can approach fixtures with foreign titans with more intensity, the Bundesliga boasts a more compelling product to pitch to foreign TV markets, the clubs earn a greater share of that revenue, which is then invested back into the academies, which continue to spawn generations of superstars. And a few other clubs can get their hands on some silverware. Theoretically, at least.

If winning the World Cup was the culmination of Germany's 10-year plan, they might need another decade-long blueprint to produce a genuine challenger to Bayern. Quite how the other clubs can afford to keep pace with the Munich giants, though, is another matter.

Because, if the gap is vast on the field, it is even wider off it – the likelihood of a club matching Bayern's expenditure is remote. Dortmund and Schalke come closest in terms of financial power, but even they lag some distance in the rear-view mirror, their wage bills barely over half of Bayern's. Beyond them, the drop-off is substantial – next wealthiest Wolfsburg's average wage was around a third of Bayern's in 2013/14. In a Premier League context, that's the wage bill of Fulham, who were actually relegated that season, achieving the league position of Arsenal.

Bayern are a regular fixture in the debate for the planet's most valuable club, while Dortmund and Schalke are competing to be the biggest in their region. Those two, the brightest hopes for some Bundesliga competition, made the top 15 of Forbes' 2015 rich list – but will likely plummet in ranking as a result of the £5.2billion Premier League TV rights deal, which will soon leave them struggling to match English clubs such as West Ham and Stoke in the transfer market, let alone mounting a serious challenge to Bayern.

With the ability to compete on the continent likely to fade, so too will the chance of challenging domestically, with players less inclined to sign for Bundesliga also-rans – and the gulf between the best, Bayern, and the rest will likely expand. Of course, it's not impossible that a batch of youngsters will emerge from the same academy and catapult a club higher – but relying on a golden generation for your league's competitiveness is not ideal. Especially as any such group would subsequently be poached by Bayern, in all probability. That's part of the way they saw off Dortmund, anyway.

But who's to say that the current crop of German stars isn't already the golden generation – and that it won't be downhill from here? The Under-21s, for instance, were thumped 5-0 in the 2015 European Championships by Portugal at the semi-final stage. Weirdly reminiscent of the seniors' deconstruction of Brazil a year earlier, Under 21 manager Horst Hrubesch admitted that he was relieved the score-line hadn't been even more convincing – so one-sided was the clash.

For former national team captain Philipp Lahm, it was perhaps a sign of softening youth players, who have been given increasing prominence throughout Germany, although their status has been handled differently to their counterparts in England.

During an interview for *BT Sport*, he said of the comparison between his time coming through the youth ranks to what players now experience: "It was a hard school definitely [during his youth] – it was a different time, but it was also beautiful.

"Times have changed now, where young players have more of a chance to come into the first team and be a part of the team. They are accepted straightaway and helped a lot more. Whether that's a good thing or not, I'm not so sure, because to push yourself through that time is something that this generation has missed out on."

Whether as a result of skipping the school of hard knocks or not, the Under 21 side, highly touted before the European Championships, underperformed in the Czech Republic. Indeed, only one member of the squad was named in the *Guardian*'s team of the tournament, Premier League based Emre Can, of Liverpool. Alongside him was England right-back Carl Jenkinson. And their last four berth sounds more flattering than it was, Germany won just one game all tournament – the 3-0 group stage victory over Denmark – drawing the other two group stage games, before losing to Portugal. Even England won a game – the only side to defeat eventual winners Sweden.

*

While there is much to applaud about German football's philosophy, that's not to say that it's perfect. Because, of course, even the best ideas don't guarantee success – there'll always be a danger of it not working out for one reason or another.

For instance, while supporter ownership – the highly praised 50+1 ruling – keeps out unreliable billionaires from takeovers, it doesn't prevent business involvement. As revealed in *Chapter 9*, three giant companies own a stake in Bayern Munich – Adidas, Audi, and Allianz. And Hoffenheim serve as an example where a businessman can get around the ruling – owner Dietmar Hopp is happy with 49% of the voting rights (but owns something like 96% of the shares) in exchange for ploughing his money in.

Similarly, energy drink giant Red Bull were able to purchase the license of third tier side SSV Markranstädt, and replace them with their own side RB Leipzig, starting in the fifth division the following season – the RB standing for RassenBallsport, but an obvious allusion to their ownership. Upon completing the takeover in 2009, it was made clear that Red Bull had a 10-year plan of their own – to reach the Bundesliga within a decade.

While the Premier League might be the most commercialised league in world football – with controversies such as the renaming of Newcastle's St James' Park to the Sports Direct Arena – even there the idea of a *club's* name effectively being sponsored is scandalous. RB Leipzig, by the way, are far from popular in Germany – but have kept to the rules, and risen to the Bundesliga 2. It seems that the rules designed to obstruct the likes of Abramovich and the Abu Dhabi Group now have loopholes.

And even those clubs that are fully supporter-owned aren't free from problems – just because you are owned by your fans, it doesn't mean there is any guarantee of smooth running. Felix Magath's reign at Schalke was beset with issues, one of which was a restriction that meant he couldn't sign a player for more than £300,000 without the approval of an 11-person supervisory board. You don't need a German saying to express Magath's frustration: it was likely a case of 'too many chefs spoil the broth'.

The £300,000 limit was part of Schalke's constitution; Magath tried to have the clause deleted, but the members voted against him. In a way, it's a safeguard against excessive spending – but, with lofty ambitions, it is fair to assert that setting the boundary so low would hamper transfer proceedings. At best, slowing them down, at worst, losing the player to a rival while they dawdle. That Magath arrived at Schalke having led Wolfsburg to the league title, and as a former Bayern boss, you'd think the club would have trusted him more.

Another issue with the domestic game is that many German players appear to have struggled when heading overseas. André Schürrle, for instance, such a key element of the World Cup winning side, failed to make a convincing mark at Chelsea, and returned to his homeland barely 18 months later. Another to struggle in West London was Marko Marin who, after a handful of unconvincing cameos, was dispatched on loan, and has remained elsewhere since.

Mesut Özil, though he has won two FA Cups with Arsenal, has often been a source of division and contention about his true quality, and whether he merited his £42.5million price tag.

*

Chapter 13

Before their 7-1 thumping of Brazil in the 2014 World Cup semi-final, Germany's report card was very different to what it became after winning. In the build up to that clash with the hosts, manager Joachim Low had to fend off criticisms of his side's style of play, insisting his only priority was to win.

But, that win against Brazil aside, the naysayers had a point – Germany's style was not eye-catching or joyous to watch, it was not the sort of football that would inspire young fans to head to their back gardens to recreate. It was a careful, guarded, dare I say 'efficient' approach.

And, yes, it worked. Would English fans be critical if the Three Lions fluked their way to a World Cup victory? No chance. But will the world champions of 2014 be remembered fondly as amongst history's great entertainers? It's equally unlikely.

No side has a duty to play attractive football but it is still a fair criticism – perhaps a downside of a plan that has been so well managed and organised is that it prompts a style of play that mirrors it.

That perceived pedestrian nature was flagged by Hannover goalkeeper Ron-Robert Zieler, when asked to compare the Bundesliga to the Premier League – with the lack of urgency in Germany revealed as a weakness. He said: "In England, the teams play more attacking football, it's a very fast game. In Germany, it's more technical and we try to keep possession a bit more than some teams there – the style is in-between Italy and England.

"It looks like the teams in England work hard. When you see the English teams, they play with a lot of passion, maybe in Germany sometimes we can learn to fight for each ball."

*

The most controversial allegations levied at the Bundesliga and German football are off field, with the suggestion that the use of crystal meth amongst fans is an issue for some clubs.

In December 2014, Dr Roland Härtel-Petri gave a lecture to German club representatives on the issue of 'drugs in the fan scene' – reporting that crystal meth was particularly popular because it increased energy and was a discreet way of entering a stadium under the influence.

Contentiously, he told German newspaper *Welt*: "Alcohol remains the main issue, but crystal meth is far from something which only appears as a one-off. The DFL is beginning to accept that."

It's common knowledge, too, amongst fans – even if only tongue-in-cheek. When Dynamo Dresden hosted Cologne in 2013, supporters held up a banner which said: 'Don't meth with Cologne? We'll blow you away', a play on the German word for snorting.

While in March of the same year Dortmund fans saw a similar banner confiscated. It read: 'Not enough money for cocaine, Nuremberg? Why else the dirty Czech muck?'

German clubs, though, deny any such issue with crystal meth or any other drugs – tending to dismiss it as a minor, societal problem.

*

A predictable domestic league and an efficient but not exhilarating national team doesn't sound like the hallmarks of an all-conquering blueprint – but perhaps these criticisms are just exceptions to the rule, or inevitable downsides to a wide selection of positives.

So, just how highly lauded should the Bundesliga blueprint be, and what lies in store for German fans and football going forward? That's the billion Euro question, and one that will be posed in the next chapter...

Chapter 14
Conclusions

There's little doubt that German football has undergone a remarkable transformation since 2000, with the development of a domestic league that is amongst the world's best – and a national side that has rediscovered not just its intimidating reputation, but an ethos and philosophy.

And the signs are that winning the World Cup in 2014 wasn't the peak of this project, but the precursor of more to come; football in Germany has never been in better health. Of course, there's no way to guarantee that they will win every international tournament for the next decade, but the legacy will be felt, and measured, more closely to home – with the continued rise of the Bundesliga.

Until fairly recently a small-fry player alongside its counterparts in England, Italy, and Spain, the top German division has come to prominence, and will soon be genuinely ready to challenge the Premier League for a global audience. Just as Serie A, La Liga and, currently, the Premier League, have enjoyed the status of the world's foremost football league, it feels like the Bundesliga's time is now.

Certainly, with the division's 'big picture' thinking – pricing, fan focus, and the like – it might have more sustainability than others that have peaked and then troughed. In Italy, for instance, Serie A has endured a difficult spell parallel to the Bundesliga's upturn.

Crucial to German football's challenge to England as the 'home' of the sport will be maintaining its admirable current approach – resisting the urge to get lost amongst the hyper-marketing and extreme revenue streams that come with the Premier League model.

While some elements will *need* to be learned from the Premier League in order to grow the Bundesliga's brand – a sickeningly corporate-sounding phrase, but a necessity of modern sport – a pinch of salt should be applied in most cases. Bayern Munich, certainly, are proving themselves adept at marketing the club in a way an English equivalent would, and Dortmund aren't far behind on that front, either. It's just up to the rest of the league to catch up.

And though the idea that, say, Frankfurt or Augsburg can become household names overseas seems unlikely, you need only look at the reputation of Stoke City five to ten years ago, and their comparative pulling power now, for inspiration. The fact that the Potters signed Bojan from Barcelona in the summer of 2014 spoke volumes.

Currently, the Premier League is wealthier and more widely watched than the Bundesliga. It will be up to officials in the German game's ruling bodies as to whether surpassing the English will be a priority for them; the new television deal should be a step towards narrowing the gap, at least, on both counts.

Keeping the focus on home-grown youth players, fan involvement, and carefully monitored ownership and debt levels, will be key distinguishing factors, too. Marketing bods might have advised that to 'break' the Far East, Manchester United needed to sign Ji-Sung Park, but international supporters, generally, are not tunnel-visioned in terms of nationality – they will obviously cheer on compatriots, but also display a similar sort of pride towards youth players at their club. The number of African fans, for instance, lamenting Manchester United's double sale of Tom Cleverley and Danny Welbeck on the club's official Facebook page was eyebrow raising; wherever they're from, supporters buy into the identity of their club, and United were betraying theirs by getting rid of starlets they'd made themselves.

In this sense, the Bundesliga will offer plenty to celebrate and football fans relish any opportunity to get one over supporters of rival clubs. While Arsenal endured a barren spell of silverware in the mid-2000s, their fans were always keen to emphasise the lack of debt their team had compared to others, especially in light of building a new stadium. Quite how this resonated with American supporters is unclear, but it did – I met many State-side Gunners that were incredibly proud of how their club funded the building of The Emirates, while still retaining Champions League football.

And it is the US that could prove the setting for the key battle between the Premier League and the Bundesliga. With 'soccer' always improving in popularity across the States, it is now the norm for

Premier League sides to flock there every pre-season, while Manchester City own a stake in MLS franchise New York City. German clubs are only just following suit – it took Bayern until April 2014 to even open a US office, undergoing their first American tour that summer. Dortmund, meanwhile, have partnered with two lower league American sides – Cincinnati United and La Roca. But Chelsea have had a tie-up with the MLS' dominant force, LA Galaxy, since 2007.

Winning the American fans is so important, because television deals there are hugely lucrative – between 2013 and 2016, the Premier League agreed a $250million deal with broadcaster NBC to show every single game. The English game has stolen a march on the market, but the Bundesliga's own US deal, starting from the 2015/16 season, means they aren't far behind.

And second place, behind the (at times) monstrous Premier League, isn't such a bad place to be. Especially with a system that allows your national team to prosper, rather than suffocate home-grown talent in favour of cheap foreign imports who might boost shirt sales in some far-flung corner of the world. The Bundesliga might not be the biggest brand in European football, but it certainly appears to offer the most balanced league.

As Christian Seifert, Bundesliga CEO, says: "We have a lot of respect for the Premier League. It has great club names, great coaches and players – but this is a completely different system.

"We think a lot about the future. The big challenge is to keep performing, at a very good, top European level, while having affordable tickets and deep roots in society. In that, we do feel we have something in the Bundesliga of which we can be a little bit proud."

Talk about hitting the nail on the head – it is exactly this approach that has left English football fans casting envious glances towards Germany, who have proved it is possible to still be successful with domestic players. With the lowest percentage of foreign stars across Europe's big five leagues in 2013, the Bundesliga produced both Champions League finalists and, a year later, the nucleus of a world-conquering squad.

As a result, German players – like the German system – are properly in vogue. Who was the player Louis Van Gaal pinpointed as essential for rebuilding Manchester United around in the summer of 2015? Germany captain Bastian Schweinsteiger, their first ever German player. Which statement signing did Arsenal splurge a club record fee on to indicate their return to title contention after almost a decade in the wilderness? Playmaker Mesut Özil, who orchestrated England's downfall at both Under 21 and senior level in the summers of 2009 and 2010.

Barcelona won the 2015 Champions League with a German, Marc-André ter Stegen, in goal. Big spending French side PSG, highlighting a problem position between their own goalposts, made a surprise swoop for Frankfurt keeper Kevin Trapp. Sami Khedira joined Juventus after their defeat by Barca in that European final, Toni Kroos is a key man at Real Madrid, Mario Gomez leads the line at Fiorentina and Lukas Podolski joined Turkish champions Galatasaray from Arsenal.

In a way that English stars rarely have, German players have prospered overseas, just as they continue to do so in their domestic league. A balance the Bundesliga as a whole continues to strike.

England and the Premier League might consider their perspective of German football as some cursory over-the-shoulder glance but, actually, if England are to prosper on an international stage again any time soon, they should be looking at the Bundesliga from behind – by following in their footsteps.

That's because the Bundesliga blueprint is the most admirable and definitive guide for a footballing culture and philosophy, where the domestic division and international side work hand-in-hand together, recognising each other's importance and contribution to the relationship.

As a plan for a league, the blueprint has few flaws, and would improve almost every other division in world football if it were applied to them. The Germans, ever the masters of engineering, have manufactured an all-conquering system once again – German football is the envy of the globe.

Other Books from Bennion Kearny

José Mourinho: The Rise of the Translator by Ciaran Kelly

From Porto to Chelsea, and Inter to Real Madrid – the Mourinho story is as intriguing as the man himself. Now, a new challenge awaits at Stamford Bridge. Covering the Mourinho story to October 2013 and featuring numerous exclusive interviews with figures not synonymous with the traditional Mourinho narrative.

"Enlightening interviews with those who really know José Mourinho" – Simon Kuper, Financial Times.

"Superb read from a terrific writer" – Ger McCarthy, Irish Examiner

What Business Can Learn From Sport Psychology: Ten Lessons for Peak Professional Performance by Dr Martin Turner & Dr Jamie Barker

It goes without saying that business performance has many parallels with sporting performance. But did you realize that the scientific principles of sport psychology, used by elite athletes the world over, are being used by some of the most successful business professionals? Performance - in any context - is about utilizing and deploying every possible resource to fulfil your potential.

With this book you will develop the most important weapon you need to succeed in business: your mental approach to performance. This book reveals the secrets of the winning mind by exploring the strategies and techniques used by the most successful athletes and professionals on the planet.

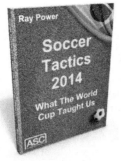

Soccer Tactics 2014: What The World Cup taught Us by Ray Power

Soccer Tactics 2014 analyses the intricacies of modern international systems, through the lens of matches in Brazil. Covering formations, game plans, key playing positions, and individuals who bring football tactics to life - the book offers analysis and insights for soccer coaches, football players, and fans the world over.

Whether it is Tiki-Taka, counter-attacking, or David defending heroically to defeat Goliath - this book sheds light on where football tactics currently stand... and where they are going.

Graduation: Life Lessons of a Professional Footballer by Richard Lee

The 2010/11 season will go down as a memorable one for Goalkeeper Richard Lee. Cup wins, penalty saves, hypnotherapy and injury would follow, but these things only tell a small part of the tale. Filled with anecdotes, insights, humour and honesty - Graduation uncovers Richard's campaign to take back the number one spot, save a lot of penalties, and overcome new challenges. What we see is a transformation - beautifully encapsulated in this extraordinary season.

The Way Forward: Solutions to England's Football Failings by Matthew Whitehouse

English football is in a state of crisis. It has been almost 50 years since England made the final of a major championship and the national sides, at all levels, continue to disappoint and underperform. Yet no-one appears to know how to improve the situation. In The Way Forward, football coach Matthew Whitehouse examines the causes of English football's decline and offers a number of areas where change and improvement need to be implemented immediately. With a keen focus and passion for youth development and improved coaching he explains that no single fix can overcome current difficulties and that a multi-pronged strategy is needed. If we wish to improve the standards of players in England then we must address the issues in schools, the grassroots, and academies, as well as looking at the constraints of the Premier League and English FA.

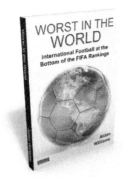

Worst in the World: International Football at the bottom of the FIFA Rankings by Aidan Williams

The fate of sporting underdogs has long stirred the passions of many a follower. There is something pleasing about watching apparently 'ordinary' people taking on the sporting elite. Teachers, accountants, fishermen and waiters – they play for the love of football and the pride in their nation.

For footballing countries ranked at the bottom of FIFA's world rankings life can be hard. Sporadic fixtures against far better equipped teams can be a soul-destroying enterprise – frequent defeat, sometimes bordering on humiliation, is the regular outcome for these teams and their players. But when that positive result finally arrives, it can mean so much: unbridled joy, national glory, and even… redemption.

In *Worst in the World*, Aidan Williams looks at the national teams at the wrong end, so to speak, of FIFA's rankings. In doing so, he brings attention to those nations whose footballing aspirations lie not in trophies or even qualification, but simply in the love of the game and the pride of representing their country.

Universality | The Blueprint for Soccer's New Era: How Germany and Pep Guardiola are showing us the Future Football Game by Matthew Whitehouse

The game of soccer is constantly in flux; new ideas, philosophies and tactics mould the present and shape the future. In this book, Matthew Whitehouse – acclaimed author of The Way Forward: Solutions to England's Football Failings - looks in-depth at the past decade of the game, taking the reader on a journey into football's evolution. Examining the key changes that have occurred since the turn of the century, right up to the present, the book looks at the evolution of tactics, coaching, and position-specific play. They have led us to this moment: to the rise of universality. Universality | The Blueprint For Soccer's New Era is a voyage into football, as well as a lesson for coaches, players and fans who seek to know and anticipate where the game of the future is heading.

See all our Football Books: **www.BennionKearny.com/soccer**

CPSIA information can be obtained
at www.ICGtesting.com
Printed in the USA
LVOW04s1146091115

461681LV00003B/249/P

9 781910 515327